How To Spot An Owl

THE HOW-TO-SPOT SERIES

How To Spot A Fox, by J. David Henry
How To Spot An Owl, by Patricia and Clay Sutton

How To Spot An Owl

Patricia and Clay Sutton

Houghton Mifflin Company
Boston   New York

Library of Congress Cataloguing-in-Publication Data

Sutton, Patricia
    How to spot an owl / Patricia and Clay Sutton.
      p.   cm. — (The How to spot series)
    Includes bibliographical references (p.   ) and index.
    ISBN 1-881527-35-2 (hard)
    ISBN 1-881527-36-0 (paper)
    1. Owls—North America. 2. Bird watching—North America.
    I. Sutton, Clay. II. Title. III. Series.
    QL696.S8S785 1994
    598.9'7'097—dc20   93-40317

Printed and bound in Canada by
Metropole Litho
St. Bruno de Montarville, Québec

Designed by Eugenie Seidenberg Delaney

Cover: A pair of barn owls / Photograph by Ron Austing

10 9 8 7 6 5 4 3

*This book is dedicated
to our mentors,
and to all mentors*

Contents

Key to Range Maps

☐ Breeding Range

☐ Permanent Range

☐ Winter Range

Note: Owl sizes (length and wingspan) are averages, since female owls (except burrowing owls) are larger than their respective males.

Acknowledgments

We owe Ed Manners and Al Nicholson, our owl mentors, and Bill Bailey, who shared so many natural history lessons and his vast library with two curious naturalists, more than we can say and more than they could ever know.

Jack Connor encouraged us to write this book and reviewed it in its entirety. Jack's knowledge as a naturalist combined with his editorial skills greatly helped to strengthen and tighten this book.

Our thanks to Katy Duffy, and David Sibley for reviewing the entire book for accuracy and its western flavor, and to Bruce Colvin, Paul Hegdal, Paul Kerlinger, Pete Dunne, Jeffery Dodge, David Evers and Kim Eckert for reviewing parts of the book that related to their region or research.

For shared owl-excursion memories, thanks to Joan Walsh and David Sibley, Rich Stallcup, Tony Leukering, Louise Zemaitis and Mitchell Smith, Alec Humann, Frank Nicoletti, Dave Wiedner, Jack and Jesse Connor, Patti Hodgetts, Jim Dowdell, Paul and Anita Guris, Jon Sutton, Jim and Dale Watson, Linda Ganassi, Bill Glaser and Dave Ward.

Tom Gilmore, director of the New Jersey Audubon Society, Paul Kerlinger, director of the Cape May Bird Observatory, and Bob Zappalorti of Herpetological Associates supported this project at every step.

We are indebted to Wendy and Dennis Allen, Paul Kenny and Danny Taylor of the Baruch Marine Laboratory, University of South Carolina, and to the Baruch Foundation for their assistance, computer time and logistical support during our sabbatical taken to write this book.

In this age when so many dream homes are built in the midst of wild areas, we would like to thank the Barbara Kozaks of the world who own wild areas and leave them wild for the owls and other wildlife.

In closing, we thank our parents, for their ongoing support and encouragement and for passing on their love of the outdoors.

A bird of the prairies, the burrowing owl is found from the Great Plains to California.

Foreword

IT WAS NIGHT, but the fields and woodlands of Cape May Point, New Jersey, had none of the qualities of night. The moon was full, bright enough to hurt the eyes. A person could read by such a light. A person could see as well as owls must see—might even, with good fortune, see an owl, either a long-eared, a barn owl or a saw-whet—the species whose migratory paths thread the Cape May peninsula.

I was prepared to stay up all night if I had to. In fact, I did stay up all night because I could not turn away from what was the most incredible night of my life—the night a host of migrating owls passed through Cape May beneath a moon so bright that the birds cast shadows on the earth.

Barn owls glowed like silver and hovered like moths. Saw-whet owls shot across open fields in ground-hugging volleys and tooted from honeysuckle tangles. Along the edge of the marsh, long-eared owls flew in silent packs of three, four and five.

I don't know how many individual owls I saw that night—more than 50 and less than 100. The number, whatever it was, is irrelevant. But from the perspective afforded by my 37 years of bird study, I can assure you that night was one of my most memorable. It all came of being in the right place at the right time and knowing how to use conditions to my advantage—knowledge you will share once you read this book.

Spotting owls requires time, practice and guidance. No fisherman is born knowing precisely where to cast a fly so it falls in the face of hungry trout. No binocular is going to fall upon a roosting saw-whet owl unless it is guided with skill.

In all of North America, there are probably no two people better suited to the task of instructing others in the art of finding owls than Pat and Clay Sutton. I say this with conviction and unrepenting bias because Pat, a co-worker at New Jersey Audubon Society's Cape May Bird Observatory, and Clay, an environmental consultant with Herpetological Associates, have been among my closest friends since 1976. I have spent hundreds of hours in the field with them. I have marveled at their field

The long-eared owl is shy, secretive and easily flushed, which makes it difficult to spot.

skills, shared many of their discoveries and benefited from their vast experience.

I have seen Pat stalking holly thickets, searching for saw-whet signs, peering into tangles for minutes on end until her eyes fused to a spot and her lips formed the words everyone was waiting to hear—"I see the bird." I have marveled, over and over again, at Clay's ability to sift the horizon through his binoculars and find short-eared owls under light conditions that would defeat the eyes of a cat.

It's not magic, it's perseverance coupled with practice and ambition. It only looks like magic—because you don't enjoy the skills yourself, not yet. But that is the purpose of this book—the Suttons wish to share the skills they have shared with so many of their other friends.

Their other talents notwithstanding, the thing I admire most about Clay and Pat is that their enthusiasm for finding owls has never eclipsed their concern for the welfare of these birds.

Pat and Clay are not just exceptional field naturalists, nor just gifted instructors. They are committed environmentalists striving to ensure that owls, and all the earth's magical creatures, command a place on a planet that is being twisted to serve our species' selfish designs. This is the most important lesson an incipient owl watcher can learn— that a concern for the welfare of birds goes hand in hand with enjoying them. Of what possible use is a talent for finding owls if there are none to find? Consider that as you read *How To Spot An Owl*.

—*Pete Dunne*

Preface

WHEN WE WERE first asked to write this book, we reacted with mixed feelings. Yes, we wanted to share the wonder of owls and how much fun it can be to search for and find them. But, on the other hand, we know that in many locations owls are threatened and declining in numbers. In many areas, their habitats are decreasing. What's more, we know of several cases where owls have been disturbed by eager owl watchers, and you will find examples of this throughout the book.

All of us are guilty. Just last summer, we found a saw-whet owl in the Cape May area, a new county record at the extreme southern limit of the species' coastal range. We certainly did not put it on the hotline. But, as most people would do, we told a friend. The friend told a friend, and that friend told a couple of other people.

A month later, we were approached by someone we barely knew, who said, "I couldn't find your saw-whet. It wouldn't answer tapes." Subsequently we learned that the bird had been "taped" by at least six different groups, some more than once. No wonder it was not calling—it had been harassed into silence, or worse, it had left the area due to the constant disturbance. While one person may do no harm, cumulative pressure can have a severe adverse impact on owls.

We have tried to write this book with the owls' welfare foremost in mind. We hope we have been successful in this effort. On the positive side, as more people learn how to spot owls, more will

In the winter, short-eared owls can be spotted throughout most of the lower 48 states.

Although relatively small in size, the pygmy owl is still an aggressive predator.

have an understanding of owls, and more will feel a need to protect them. Often, discovery can lead directly to protection efforts. In many areas throughout our country, so little is known about owl status and distribution that their conservation is in its infancy. More interest means more data, more data means greater knowledge, and greater knowledge can result in better conservation efforts.

There is no group of birds, except possibly rails, about which so little is known as the owl group. To paraphrase something naturalist Henry Beston once said, owls hear different voices, voices we cannot even begin to perceive, and act and interact in ways that we diurnal creatures will never witness, nor ever understand fully. We can study them, we can learn to spot them, but, at least to us, owls will always remain aloof, apart, mysterious.

We share with you the lessons we have learned while owling over the last 20 years. We have tried to pass on these lessons, methods, places and timing. We hope we have captured and conveyed the magic of owling. May this book inspire you to go out for owls. We hope they will be there for you too.

—*Pat and Clay Sutton*

Part One:
An Introduction to Owling

Owling Basics

A RECENT SURVEY LINE cut through the woods. One of its casualties was a huge pine. Although virtually hidden by the felled tree, a promising dab of white caught Pat's eye. On hands and knees, she crawled under the downed tree for a better look. As her eyes adjusted to the small, dark inner room formed by the branches, she saw before her a pool of whitewash and several tiny pellets. Barely breathing, she slowly lifted her head

Found throughout the continent, the great horned owl, *above and previous pages*, is also the most abundant owl in many areas. *Right:* a saw-whet owl.

and was eye to eye with a fully alert, wide-eyed saw-whet owl, elongated and looking intently for signs of further danger. At once she slowly backed out. While still on her knees, she could look through the lacy needles and branches into the saw-whet's inner sanctuary from a less threatening distance.

It was the second saw-whet Pat had ever seen; the first had been shown to us by Ed Manners, New Jersey's owl "mystic," just a week before. Until that visit with Ed, Pat had doubted that we would ever find a saw-whet in the wild. Although hundreds migrate through Cape May Point, New Jersey, each fall, up until now we had searched for them in vain.

Ed's intimate knowledge of saw-whets was based on more than 30 years of study. A day afield with this owl expert was worth lifetimes of studying books. We learned of signs that give away an owl's presence. The gleaming white owl excrement, known as whitewash, often drips like candle wax down through the branches of a favorite roost tree, though sometimes a pile of pellets—

An owl's flattened facial disc, such as the great gray's, reflects sounds to the bird's ears.

the regurgitated, indigestible parts of an owl's prey (fur or feathers, skull and bones)—is the only clue. Ed also taught us how difficult it is to see an owl even when it is in plain view. Their preference for perching with a branch partially obscuring them successfully breaks up their overall shape and is an ingenious camouflaging technique (see photograph on page 17).

That day and each owl experience since have added to our confidence that owls are all around us. They can't always be found, but they are there, awaiting discovery.

Owling is a learned activity: you can only be successful after much reading about the subject, priceless time spent with owl experts, hours afield, many owlless outings and sometimes years of searching.

Even to a seasoned owler, it may take some time to get into the right frame of mind for a successful day's owling. The mind needs to be emptied out—tasks and distractions must be forgotten. You must be fully focused on the owly woods you're exploring. Every tree needs to be checked from every angle for possible stick nests or nest cavities; it is amazing how these can seem to simply not exist until the perfect angle makes one visible. The ground under all possible perches needs to be searched for pellets and whitewash, and that normally means every evergreen (holly, cedar, pine, honeysuckle tangle and laurel) and every large-spreading deciduous tree. Every sound may be an owl and must be noted—sometimes the only clue to an owl's presence is a wing hitting a branch as the owl drops from its perch and glides away, silent and unseen.

If you don't find owls at first, do not get discouraged. In the early stages of our owling careers, one owler shared these words of wisdom with us: "You never seem to see or find what you are looking for, but quite often you discover something just as interesting and exciting. And you certainly won't ever find what you are looking for if you don't go out and look." Think of owling as a wonderful excuse to be outdoors!

The quarry

MOST OWLS are nocturnal, although a few are crepuscular, meaning they are active during the dim hours of dawn and dusk or on overcast days. By day, nocturnal owls perch or roost where they can't be seen. If they are found, they may be harassed by songbirds or crows or they may fall victim to predators. A favorite roost site might be in a dense evergreen or honeysuckle tangle, in a niche along a cliff or canyon wall, camouflaged up against a tree trunk, in a hollow tree or man-made owl nest box, in a tus-

sock of tall marsh grass or even on a rooftop.

As dusk settles, owls move out from the deep woods or secluded areas where they've spent the day in hiding and fly to an edge overlooking a good feeding site. This often happens at last light, when humans can barely see. The owl looks like nothing more than a headless form against the horizon, often sitting on the highest perch available—a dead snag, a cliff ledge, a rock promontory or a duck blind. The hunt begins immediately. The owl's body remains motionless, but its head is constantly turning as it watches, listens and triangulates

Owls have the ability to rotate their heads up to 270 degrees to locate prey. *Above*, a short-eared owl.

on the location of its prey.

In order to hunt successfully at night, owls have evolved in unique ways. Since they depend on their hearing to locate prey, owls have very large, wide heads to accommodate their huge, highly developed ears. The ears of most owls are arranged asymmetrically (with one higher than the other) so they can triangulate on their prey.

When an owl hears potential prey, such as a mouse rustling through the grass, it begins to bob its head up and down and to slide it from side to side while its body remains stationary. This head movement tells the owl exactly where the prey is. To further enhance their hearing, most owls have a flattened facial disc that reflects sound to their ears, much in the way that a satellite dish is able to pull in television signals.

This sensitive hearing can enable an owl to detect prey under incredible circumstances. One of our most vivid memories is of a great gray owl successfully hunting on a snowy winter day. It was perched high in a dead snag. Alert, its head snapped this way and that as its ears detected potential prey—prey that was not at all obvious in the white landscape of deep snow.

Each time it singled out potential prey, the owl extended its thick, feathered neck and turned its full facial disc in that direction for what seemed like a better "listen." Then it left the perch and flew silently in a low direct line toward the spot, at least 150 feet away. At the last moment, it suddenly and ungracefully flopped down into the

A snowy owl attacks a mouse. An owl's hearing is so acute it can detect prey under snow.

two-foot-deep snow, chest first. Its wings were extended and its tail fully spread, its body pressed down on the snow. It heaved its body weight up and down. After several moments, in one case, it sat up with a vole in its talons, quickly transferred it to its bill, and swallowed it in two gulps, head first with the tail dangling out momentarily before disappearing.

Owls see perfectly well in daylight, and 10 to 100 times better than humans in dim light. Their large eyes are set in front of their skull, unlike most other birds, whose eyes are set on each side of the head. Forward-facing eyes give the owl two overlapping fields of vision (binocular vision) and greater depth perception. But an owl's eyes are fixed, immovable in their sockets. In order to see to either side, an owl must turn its entire head. Extra vertebrae in their necks permit owls' heads to rotate up to 270 degrees in either direction—almost all the way around.

Owls fly and glide in total silence. This is possible because their feathers, wings and legs are structured so there are no hard edges to cause wind resistance. Owl feathers have a soft, velvety covering. The leading edge of each primary wing feather is fluted or serrated to muffle sound as the wing passes through the air. On most owls, even the legs and feet are feathered so the extended

The flight of a hunting owl, such as this great gray, *top*, is silent. One explanation is that the serrated wing feathers, *bottom*, muffle sound.

talons make a soundless approach. Silent flight allows an owl to completely surprise its prey and also prevents its movements from interfering with or muffling prey detection. An owl's silent flight often enables it to flush unobserved and disappear from an area where you know it has been.

Owls have wide wings and lightweight bodies, which helps them to fly silently.

The ear tufts of this long-eared owl have nothing to do with hearing; they provide camouflage.

The flight of smaller owls appears moth-like and buoyant. In between intermittent flapping, they glide on bowed or slightly drooping wings. Hawks, in contrast, often glide on flat or slightly raised wings.

An owl in flight and perched appears headless—its large head merges with the body as one tubular shape. Hawks, in comparison, appear to have small heads on fairly blocky bodies.

Owls are very elusive and secretive. They are usually extremely well camouflaged—many have a streaked or barred chest that blends with the tree bark. The "ear tufts" have nothing to do with hearing, but add to the owl's overall camouflage by breaking up its shape. An owl's ability to go from a plump shape to a very elongated shape when alarmed also helps camouflage the owl by making it look like a tree stump or part of a branch.

Owls' feet have a wide spread and the outer toe is highly movable, so wiggling prey cannot escape. The size of the talon is indicative of the size of the preferred prey. For example, great horned owls' enormous, piercing talons enable them to take very large prey: muskrat, opossum, skunk, rabbit and even young fox. Barn owls, with medium-sized talons, usually prey on rats, mice and voles. Saw-whets, with small talons, favor mice, shrews and insects.

Owls normally eat their prey whole, although if the prey is too large to be swallowed whole, they use their hooked beaks to tear it apart. The nutrients are absorbed in the stomach, and the undigested prey parts that are hard and of little nutritional value (bones, bills, teeth, skulls and feathers or fur) are compressed into pellets and regurgitated through the mouth in compact masses rather than excreted as feces.

Owls usually eat their prey whole. Any undigested parts are compressed into pellets and regurgitated.

Since owls usually swallow their prey whole, their pellets often contain the entire skeleton. By contrast, since hawks normally pull their prey apart, pulling off the fur or feathers before eating the meat, their pellets do not contain as complete a skeleton or as much fur or feathers as the owls' do when pieced together.

Perhaps you have found "fairy rings" of feathers in the woods left by a predator; these are usually attributable to hawks and not to owls, again because owls normally swallow their prey whole. Pellets are clean, odorless and not dangerous to handle. Dissect one to learn what an owl has eaten. By studying the skull and teeth, you can often determine the species of prey.

Owls regurgitate about two pellets each day, one at their daytime roost and one at their nighttime feeding site. A pellet is regurgitated about 6½ hours after the meal. By counting the pellets under a roost site, you can determine approximately how long the owls have been using the roost.

Because they are efficient rodent predators, owls can be extremely beneficial. A barn owl, for example, eats about three mice a night. In a year, that adds up to about 1,000 mice. A pair of barn owls with young makes an even bigger dent in the rodent population.

Owls do not build their own nests. Those owls that prefer to nest out in the open will usually use an old hawk, crow, raven, magpie or squirrel nest, either in a tree, in a cactus or on a cliff ledge. Many owls, particularly the smaller ones, nest in a natural cavity or an abandoned woodpecker hole. Barn owls may use hollow trees for nest sites, but will also nest on ledges in

abandoned buildings, silos, water towers and barns—hence their name. Burrowing owls nest in abandoned animal burrows, and several species are attracted to man-made nest boxes.

The quest

THE AUTOMATIC COFFEE POT had been set to brew at 2:00 a.m. Its aroma permeated the house as we struggled into the many layers of clothing we had set out the night before when we were a bit more alert: long underwear, wool socks, turtlenecks, jeans and wool sweaters. Waiting in the car were down jackets, outer parkas, wool scarves and hats and gloves. We arrived at our first stop by 3:00 a.m. The thermometer on the bank in Dennisville read 16 degrees Fahrenheit. It was cold, but very still, windless and clear—perfect for hearing owls. It was New Year's Day and we were censusing for the Cumberland County, New Jersey, Annual Christmas Bird Count.

It was dark and would be for some time. We had to depend on our hearing to record the first three hours of birds. One of us walked along a railroad right-of-way while the other headed down a dirt road. Each of us began imitating owl calls to elicit some response from the wintering owl population. We started with a barred owl's "Who cooks for you, who cooks for you allllllll?" We hooted softly for about 15 minutes, interspersing it with silent stretches when we listened for a response. We heard nothing, but to distract us from the cold, we kept telling ourselves there were lots of owls out there. We had counted as many as five barred owls at this spot during past Christmas Bird Counts and nothing much had changed to force them out of the area.

Not moving, we tried for saw-whet owls next by imitating their repetitive tootlike call, again interspersing it with silent stretches. Still nothing, so we began to try for screech owls by whistling their low, eerie

Owls do not build nests. Some, like the great horned, *left*, use other species' stick nests. Others, like screech owls, *above*, use existing cavities.

Although they usually give a tooting call, saw-whets occasionally emit a catlike whine.

whinny or wail. Almost immediately something responded with a catlike whine. We heard it again, but couldn't place it. It sounded like something between a cat and a yellow-bellied sapsucker, and it sounded close. We scanned the tree our mystery seemed to be calling from with our flashlight and there, encased in a red cedar, sat a saw-whet owl. The call was new to us and not like anything we'd ever read about. The excitement of our discovery fueled us for the rest of the day. How many saw-whets had we overlooked up to this point by dismissing this odd call? No one we talked to after the count was familiar with this call or had linked such a call to a saw-whet. What a find and what a surprise! Since then, we have discovered saw-whets because of our familiarity with this odd call.

As we headed back to the car, whispering back and forth about other outings when we may have heard this same call, the barred owls finally let loose a cacophony of calls from the deep swamp. A good half hour had passed since we'd imitated their hooting and we had almost missed them. Typical! Patience is rewarded, however. Go with your instincts—if you feel owls should be there, wait for them.

Know your subject

SPOTTING OWLS is a challenge. It takes patience, commitment and a great deal of time. Consider yourself lucky if you actually see an owl one out of the ten times you try. Be happy with hearing them and knowing that they are there and that one of these times you will see them. Each time you succeed, you add another search image to your knowledge. Until the day you see a saw-whet owl hidden behind a cluster of holly leaves or merged with the delicate woven tangle of honeysuckle vines, you will walk by dozens.

Learn which owls are found in the area where you live or where you will be traveling. The easiest place to start is with a checklist of birds, available at most national parks, state parks and nature centers, which lists each of the birds, their seasonality and their status during each season (common, uncommon or rare).

Owlers are also very fortunate today to have a wide selection of bird field guides and treatises on owls available. At the end of this book, we have listed our favorite owl books and tapes and records of owl calls.

Field guides are indispensable for the traveling birder/owler. They include range maps and concise descriptions of each owl species—its flight, its call, its preferred habitat and often whether or not it is migratory.

The serious owler must study and learn to recognize the various owl calls, as owls are often detected only by means of their calls. Many records, tapes and compact discs now available make this task possible—all you have to do is study the various calls and commit them to memory. Expect to be surprised. The great horned owl, often referred to as the "hoot owl," has given all owls the reputation of hooting their calls or songs. Actually very few owls "hoot." Some owls screech (barn owls), others yip and bark like a dog (long-eared and short-eared owls) and the confusingly named eastern screech owl whistles a mournful wail.

Learn from the experts

WHILE YOU MAY BE LUCKY enough to have a chance encounter with an owl while looking for other things, to see owls with any regularity you need to head out and look specifically for them. To increase your chances of success, why not go looking with people who know what they are looking for? Whenever an opportunity arises to learn from an expert, take advantage of it.

Nature centers, nature clubs, bird clubs and bird observatories sometimes offer "owl prowls" or guided walks. These outings are normally led by a local owl expert and

include visits to spots where owls are likely to occur. Take advantage of these programs—they are an excellent introduction to the basics—where to go, when to go, how to look, how to listen and how to identify the various owl calls.

Owls may be a bit easier to locate during certain seasons when they congregate. Areas well known for their hawk concentrations during the spring or fall migration are often migrant traps for owls as well. For instance, the Cape May Bird Observatory offers night watches and sunset bird walks at the peak of the fall migration (September through mid-November) since many species, such as shorebirds, warblers, sparrows, herons, egrets and owls, migrate through the night rather than during daylight hours.

Whitefish Point Bird Observatory in Michigan, a spring migrant trap, offers evening flight watches from mid-April to mid-May to observe owls, particularly long-eared owls (though great gray and great horned owls have also been seen), as they leave their daytime roosts to begin their nocturnal migrations. Braddock Bay Raptor Research, on the south shore of Lake Ontario near Rochester, New York, offers owl walks at dusk every weekend from mid-March through April.

Owls are always a possibility, but certainly not guaranteed on night walks. Night outings expose you to a time when the average person has gone indoors, and they may teach you to fully use and learn from your sense of hearing, especially at dusk.

More than 1,500 National Audubon Society Christmas Bird Counts are held across North America. There is undoubtedly one held near where you live. Learn whom to contact from a local bird club or nature center, or write to *American Birds* at 700 Broadway, NY, NY 10003 (212-979-3000).

Many states have produced or are working on a breeding bird atlas. Most atlases take four to five years to complete. Find out if such a project is in progress in your state and how to get involved. If the atlas in your state has been completed and published, buy a copy. Atlas maps will clearly show you the status and distribution of each species of owl in your state.

Birding hotlines have taped announcements covering the previous week's bird sightings; nearly every state has at least one. Many hotlines are sponsored by nature centers or bird clubs. Get in the habit of regularly calling the birding hotline in your area. It will alert you to the seasonal changes in the local bird populations and to anything out of the ordinary.

Hotlines normally give information only on owl species that are not threatened by widespread knowledge of their whereabouts. Snowy owls and short-eared owls usually hunt way out over the salt marsh or farmland, and are generally undisturbed by observers on the edges of these habitats. But you will probably only rarely learn of saw-whet owl or long-eared owl roost sites, since these can be easily disrupted by eager birders.

Concentrations of species such as barn owls, *left*, gather during fall migrations.

Owling on Your Own

OWLS ARE very mysterious. Finding and actually seeing an owl is difficult even after years of successfully discovering owls. The more you learn about them, the more you will appreciate their mystique and the easier it will be to accept an owlless outing.

When you first begin your search for owls, seek out the most common owls in your area. Learn all you can from these owls, so that you can later apply what you have learned to less common owls.

We began our study of owls with the great horned, one of the largest owls. Since it is the most common owl and found in good numbers throughout most of North America, it may be the one you want to begin with too.

Great horned owls are crepuscular and come out to forest edges before full darkness and may linger until dawn. They often perch on treetops or utility poles and might be found silhouetted in the last light of day or dawn's first light. They also use an open platform-type nest rather than a hole nest inside a hollow tree or other structure, and are therefore quite a bit easier to find during the nesting season.

Great horneds are our earliest nesting bird—they nest and raise their young in the late winter months. If there are evergreens in the area, you will most likely find nests in them, but if the area is without evergreens, the nest may be quite visible in a decidu-

Great horned owls, *left*, are active at both dusk and dawn and, like other crepuscular owls, can be found silhouetted in the fading light, *above*.

ous tree that won't develop leaves until the nesting season is over. Because of their nesting habits, you may have a far easier time finding great horned owls than almost any of the other owls.

At dusk in the mid-Atlantic states from mid-September through the winter, great horned owls seem to be everywhere—their hooting calls drift across fields, over meadows and from the edge of nearly every woodlot. They often set up territories by late fall. During this time, the male calls to ward off all other males from his turf. Listen for the female answering; her call is a lower, briefer and more seductive "whoo whoo." (Some authorities disagree, saying the female initiates the hooting sessions and has the longer call.) By late January or early February the female calls from the nest.

To seek owls, use an owl's own hunting methods: At dawn or through the night when you hear the female calling, try to triangulate on the nest by listening from several different vantage points. Once you think you know the nest's general location, choose daylight hours with good visibility and move in slowly and quietly. Stop frequently, each time searching for stick nests. Stay alert for any movement or signs of owl activity. A mob of crows or jays may mean there is a male owl on vigil nearby. Study each stick nest, no matter how insignificant. Owls cannot always be choosy. Because they do not build their own nests, they have to make do with whatever is available.

While studying potential nests, look for any sign of use. Something as simple as a downy feather caught in the nest edge may mean activity. In the early stages, the female crouches way down in the nest. Often she is completely hidden. If you are lucky, her ear tufts may barely show above the nest edge. Once the young hatch and begin to grow, their bulk keeps her from being able to

If nests in evergreens are not available, great horned owls may use nests in deciduous trees.

By the end of the nesting season, owlets begin to branch away from the nest site.

hide down in the nest and she begins to sit higher up and becomes more visible. Soon the young will be large and able to protect themselves, and she will roost elsewhere. By mid-April in New Jersey (late May to early June in colder areas) the downy young are so large that they cannot hide down in the nest. At this point, they are the easiest to find and see. The first hatched is often much larger than the younger ones.

Young great horned owls are very active, moving and hopping around within the nest and on its edge. Since owls neither build nor maintain their nest, it soon begins to break down with all this activity. Some-

times by the end of the nesting season, when the young are ready to fledge, there is very little left of the actual nest structure.

By late April, the young begin to "branch" before they can actually fly, and may stray from the nest. Branching is the term given to the time when young owls cannot yet fly, but are able to test their wings a bit and hop from branch to branch. At this point, they begin to get harder to find. By mid-May, when their flight feathers grow in, the young can fly and they become very difficult, if not impossible, to find. The alert owler might still keep track of the young by listening for their loud food-begging screeches as dusk approaches. Food begging continues through the summer and sometimes into the fall.

The magic owl hours

BEGIN YOUR QUEST for owls by adjusting your schedule and your senses to the magic owl hours: the hour leading up to and the hour following dusk. At dusk, when the rest of the world is closing doors and windows, owls are becoming more alert—they become active and fly out to edges to begin their "day," and often they become vocal. Dawn can be just as productive, so choose whichever time period is more convenient for you.

You can maximize your time during these magic owl hours in several ways. Begin by taking walks at dusk in areas that are likely to host owls. Even though owls are in the deepest cover by day, most of them roost in close proximity to open habitats that are good for hunting and come out to edges overlooking these open areas at dusk. Passive listening near good feeding habitat at dusk, when owls are most vocal, can alert you to their presence. This will be far more productive leading up to and during the breeding season, when owls are most vocal. You can also cruise by car through likely habitats at dusk—stop frequently to listen for their calls and scan snags and treetops on wooded edges of fields, meadows and marshes for silhouettes. A bicycle is ideal for road cruising, as it will make it easier to hear owls calling.

An owl's silhouette will appear head-less—a big lump. In comparison, a hawk's silhouette is a small head on a blocky body. If you are fortunate enough to discover an owl that has come out to its favored evening perch, be patient and watch it. Eventually, it will begin to hunt. Unfortunately, this often happens when it is so dark that you can barely see.

A tripod-mounted telescope is helpful since you can keep your hands warm and simply keep an eye to the scope. Telescopes are more powerful than binoculars, but they let in far less light. Some of the more expensive telescopes have better light-gathering capabilities, but binoculars with good light-gathering capabilities are also invaluable to owl seekers. Once you have discovered an owl at its evening perch, return as frequently as you can during the magic owl hours and you will probably find that your bird uses the same perch or a nearby perch on most evenings.

Actively lure in owls

IT MAY BE MORE APPEALING to lure in an owl when visibility is good, either at dusk or when the moon is full. Yet a dark night works just fine and really puts you into the owl's world.

It takes a special effort and focus for humans to understand and experience the night. We need to learn to be quiet and we need to learn how to listen. Many night sounds are faint or distant, but they might be valuable clues when scouting for owls. Like an owl, learn to turn your head this way and that to locate and more directly

An owl silhouette is headless, *left*; a hawk's, *right*, has a small head on a blocky body.

face an unknown sound. Also try cupping your hands behind your ears to direct the sound.

Remember the owl's incredible hearing ability. Only talk in whispers (if at all), and keep clothing and shoe-scuffing noises to a minimum. Wear clothing that will not be noisy when you put your cold hands into your pockets or need to reach for a tissue or your binoculars. Choose a good vantage point and remain as still as possible while attempting to lure in owls. Let the owl hear nothing but what you intend it to hear.

Owls are opportunistic predators and are nearly always drawn to easy prey. An injured animal—a squeaking mouse or a squealing rabbit—is like a magnet to an owl. You can imitate an animal's distress call by squeaking. We've had good luck by loudly sucking or kissing the side of our thumb or index finger, the more ear-piercing the better because the sound will carry. Practice and see what sounds best to you.

Remember to vary the squeaks; in the wild an injured animal surely makes a variety of pained squeals. Prerecorded predator-call tapes of injured rabbits have been reported to work for owls, but are too loud and incessant for our taste. Besides, squeaking yourself works just fine.

If owls are nearby, they often respond quickly to squeaking. Your chances of seeing the owl will be far better if you squeak from a hidden position, crouched down within tall grasses, inside a car or from a true observation blind. It is important to intersperse the squeaking with silent stretches for listening and watching. Owls have noiseless flight, but sometimes call to one another while hunting.

Owls such as this great gray are opportunistic predators and are drawn to easy prey.

If the visibility is good, you may be lucky enough to see a silent and ghostly owl shape flapping directly toward you. Hold still and try not to flinch. We have had owls hover over us looking down for what they thought was their next meal. Silently watch and drink in this spectacle; you will not usually be this fortunate. Do not tease the owl by continuing to squeak.

Another active search technique is to use a tape player and play recordings of the owl's call or whistle your own imitation. This form of active luring is to be used with extreme caution because it can be very detrimental to the owls during the breeding season. It is also illegal and strictly forbidden at all times of year in some areas, such as Higbee Beach Wildlife Management Area near Cape May, New Jersey; Cave Creek Canyon in Arizona; Everglades National Park in Florida; all other National Parks (where it is considered "wildlife harassment"); and many state parks.

Tape playing is also illegal in many places that attract large numbers of birders. These tape recordings are banned for the benefit of the birds. In the Everglades, a barred owl nesting territory written up in James Lane's *Birder's Guide to Florida* had attracted hundreds of birders, many armed with taped recordings of barred owls. One day the barred owl, with young in the nest, had had enough and reacted to a recording by flying in and raking the birder with its talons.

This individual then sued the National Park! An owl's only form of defense and protection of its young is to try to frighten off an intruder, and that is just what the barred owl did. Adult owls will defend their territory and their young against any intruders, including humans. (Please read "Owling Etiquette," page 61.)

Tape recordings or imitations are often used during Christmas Bird Counts. This luring method is far less hazardous to owls if used outside the breeding season. For best results, try to break up your obvious silhouette by crouching down or by backing up to a tree or tall vegetation. Acclimate your eyes to the dark, then begin calling softly or playing the recording at a low volume. Loud is not better.

Try to make it sound as realistic as possible. Setting a tape recorder up with an endless loop and playing the call over and over again or whistling your imitation incessantly is not very realistic. Play the recording sparingly and softly for about three to five minutes, followed by about three to five minutes of quiet. Repeat this sequence about three or four times. Owls may respond almost immediately, often within five minutes. They may even respond during daylight hours, but dark, still nights are best, for the sound carries easily.

Once the owl responds, imitate its call, but do this only infrequently. You will probably learn more by listening quietly. The owl may answer with an unfamiliar sound. Or, the visitor may be a nosy owl that has come in to check out another species. The owl may fly in silently to investigate, not calling back right away or at all.

You need to be very alert for movement. Once you hear a response, watch for movement or a silhouette against the sky. If the bird is close, try to find the owl in your flashlight beam. Some owls will sit quietly, almost demurely, in the beam of a light, seemingly oblivious to how visible they are.

If the bird continues to call but is just out of view beyond dense brush, try to coax it out with soft, infrequent calling and by moving slowly and quietly away from the dense brush to a more open viewing area. Keep its interest, but don't overdo it with incessant calling. Patience, remaining quiet and still and focusing your total attention on the responding owl should ultimately pay off.

Always remember that you are the intruder. You have entered an owl's territory. Their defense may mean diving on the intruder, no matter what the season. You may wish to wear a hat and eyeglasses for protection, just in case the owl taps you on the head.

Daytime roost sites

THE NEXT STEP in your quest of owls is to discover their daytime roost sites. Go out on your own as frequently as possible in search of owls. This time will be well spent. Even if you come home owlless, you will learn how to get into an owly frame of mind.

Since most owls have incredible hearing, owling is usually more successful if done with at most one other owl enthusiast. A bunch of people or even a chatting few will probably not see owls.

You need to learn to move through the woods very quietly so that you do not scare away the owls before you have a chance to

A solid form hidden in the otherwise lacy branches of a tree is often the first sign of a roosting owl.

sight them. Each footstep needs to be as well placed and soundless as possible. Otherwise you will sound like something crashing through the woods, and the owl will silently flush away long before you find it. On a number of Christmas Bird Counts one of us, separated from the other, has seen an owl that the other has inadvertently and unknowingly flushed.

Where do you look when you walk through the woods? At your feet, lost in thought, but hoping not to trip? Or are you so distracted by your inner thoughts that you walk blindly, oblivious to your surroundings, not paying attention, and re-

membering very little about what's around you? This is the first mistake if you are out for owls. Look ahead and around. Any evergreen or tangle is a potential owl roost. Stop regularly and study the trees around you. Look for anything out of place: a stick nest, a hole in a tree trunk, a downy feather blowing from a branch or a solid form in the otherwise lacy tree branches. You must be very alert—constantly shift your focus from up into the trees, looking for a solid form, to down on the ground, searching for whitewash and pellets. As you continue, study your finds from different angles until you are sure you can dismiss them as unimportant.

Are you in a hurry when you walk through the woods? Do you see it as exercise and end up marching through the landscape? If so, this is your second mistake. Move slowly, carefully and as silently as possible. Be alert for movement.

Even if you take all these precautions, an owl is likely to see you long before you are aware of it, and it will probably flush before you are anywhere near it. By frequently stopping and looking ahead through the forest, you may detect the movement and get a glimpse of an owl flushing silently away. Often they do not fly very far. It is too dangerous for an owl to be out in the open during daylight hours, as they are out of their element and easily victimized.

So, if you see an owl flush, move ahead with even more caution as you may see it again. Sometimes when an owl is leaving a perch, its wing hits a branch. In quiet woods, with all your energy focused on owl clues, you will come to learn this sound.

In winter, certain owls are quite gregarious and roost communally, perhaps for safety. This is particularly true of short-eared, long-eared and barn owls, and occasionally saw-whet owls. Short-eared owl winter roosts are normally on the ground—out on the marsh or in fallow farm fields. Communal roosts of long-eared, barn and saw-whet owls are often in the deepest cover, but quite close to adjacent open habitats good for hunting.

If you are a city dweller, look near dumps, overgrown landfills, cemeteries, city parks, botanical gardens and golf courses. Each of these habitats is a rodent supermarket, come nightfall. Farther out in rural areas, any of the above habitats along with fields, meadows and marshes are prime hunting grounds for wintering owls, and roosts should be nearby.

Barn and long-eared owls often roost in the darkest and densest, but not necessarily the tallest, clusters of evergreens—sometimes there are up to five birds in one tree. If one should flush, look for others hidden in the tree before moving another step.

Long-eared owls often, but not always, perch right next to the trunk of a densely leaved tree. When alarmed, they tend to freeze and hide by fully elongating their

In winter, certain owls, such as long-eareds, roost communally in areas of deep cover.

posture, which makes them look like part of the tree. Even their ear tufts become fully erect. We've seen them close their eyelids almost completely, perhaps to help in their camouflage. If you are very still and quiet, they may settle back down and resume their relaxed, plump shape. Or, if you move too close, too fast, they will flush suddenly. Because long-eared owls have a tendency to flush only at close range, they may be roosting right next to a house or workplace without the residents or employees knowing.

These communal roosting owls often have a fidelity to a particular wintering site and may return again and again over a period of years to the same group of trees or the very same roost tree. In some parts of the country, where pines and cedars are not available, owls often communally roost in winter in live oaks, large cottonwoods, willows, eucalyptus and rows of planted palm trees right in towns.

Do not disturb an owl roost. If you discover one, return very infrequently. We keep tabs on a number of winter roosts in our area and have maintained population data for many years now. We never visit a particular roost more than once every three to four weeks in the winter. This rate, used with the cautions described above, seems to not cause undue disturbance.

Refrain from telling others about roosts you have discovered. Make the roost your

When alarmed, long-eared owls fully elongate their bodies and become completely motionless. After danger passes, they resume their relaxed, plump shape, *left.*

"own." It is cumulative disruption that drives owls from favored roosts. More people means more talk, more noise, more distraction and fewer owls. Owls choose a particular roost site over other sites for reasons we do not know or understand. Driving owls away from their favored roost to another less desirable roost may expose them to predators.

Owls do sometimes have alternate roost sites, however. Near our home, if long-eareds are not in their favored grove, we can usually find them in one or two other nearby evergreen stands. They may alternate between roosts on a fairly regular basis, so be flexible. If the owls are not in their customary spot, expand your search to nearby likely sites.

Hunt for owl signs

SINCE OWLS are so secretive, your search for their daytime roosts often means looking down for telltale signs as much as looking up for the well-hidden owl. Beneath an owl's favorite perch, whitewash and sometimes pellets accumulate.

An owl's excrement is called whitewash. It is very white, thick and cakey—unmistakable once you are familiar with it. The novice may easily mistake pine sap for owl whitewash as both drip down a pine trunk and gather on the forest floor. Pine sap, however, is not cakey-white like true owl whitewash. Do not be confused by songbird whitewash: it has black streaks running through it and is not solid white. Hawk whitewash appears to be sprayed over a

Small owls use the same perch day after day. After a time, their highly visible whitewash and pellets collect on lower branches and the ground.

branches below and the trunk or the ground. It is surprising how visible this whitewash can be. We've spotted it from a distance, then looked through binoculars at the tree and found an extremely camouflaged owl that otherwise would never have been seen.

On a Christmas Bird Count, we once discovered a lone long-eared owl roosting in a large holly. Our clue was what looked like a gallon of white paint poured down the trunk and onto the base of the tree. The owl was perched directly over the spot, snug up against the trunk. The owl came back to this tree the following winter as well, and to this day there are still faint signs of the whitewashed trail down the trunk. So, the next time you find owl whitewash, do not forget to look up, slowly—the owl may be right overhead.

The last thing you want to do is flush an owl before you've even seen it or had a chance to study it. Binoculars give you the necessary edge to detect an owl or signs of its presence before you flush it by moving too close. As soon as you discover a positive sign of an owl's presence, no matter how seemingly insignificant, stop where you are. Slowly lift the binoculars to your eyes and thoroughly follow up the clue. Study every branch above whitewash and pellets, look for any sign of active use at a stick nest and carefully study any solid forms in the lacy network of tree branches.

large area; owl whitewash collects directly below an owl's perch.

The smaller owls return to a perch day after day. After a period of time, their whitewash drips like white candle wax down through the branches and collects on

When you find an owl, slowly sink to the ground so that you appear less threatening. Upon discovery, the owl will no doubt be fully alert and fully elongated in its alarm posture. Wait until it relaxes and shifts into a more plump shape before considering moving. If your view is blocked and you need to move for a better look, wait until the owl is relaxed. You can't be in a rush to see an owl. Once the owl has relaxed you can move, very slowly. Move laterally for a better view, rather than forward, if at all possible.

If the bird resumes the alarm pose, stop and wait. Always keep in mind your goal: to study the owl. Once you have had a chance to fully examine the owl and are satiated, back away slowly, keeping low. When you are well away from the owl, and ideally even hidden from it by an obstruction like a tree, then rise to your feet. If you leave the owl un-alarmed, there is a good chance you can return to this daytime roost and study it again. In order not to scare the bird away, you should wait a few weeks before returning.

Owl pellets are a true treasure for the owl seeker. They might indicate a daytime roost or a nighttime feeding station. Pellets remain intact for nearly an entire season, but time and rainfall eventually break them down.

Winter roosts that attract numbers of owls year after year are particularly fun for the pellet seeker. Over time, the forest floor

Often the first sign of a well-hidden long-eared owl is the whitewash below its perch.

in these active roosts ends up covered with rodent skulls, as the pellets erode away. A few skulls on the forest floor in summer have alerted us to winter roost sites.

If you are fortunate enough to know the identity of the owl whose pellet you've discovered, it is a terrific learning experience. Start a collection of pellets, labeling the owl associated with each. You'll begin to see size patterns and you'll soon be able to recognize which species of owl was responsible for the discovered pellets.

Saw-whet and screech owl pellets are quite tiny and are often found intact under a favorite roost site. They can be as small as the top third of your index finger. Each are about the same size and often difficult to tell apart.

Long-eared and barn owl pellets are medium-sized and often dark in color. Usually found intact on the ground beneath a roost, they are about the same size and sometimes difficult to tell apart. They can be either elongated or oval and are about the length of your thumb, but twice as wide.

Great horned owl pellets, if found intact, are huge. They can fill the palm of your hand and are often pale gray in color. In coastal areas, you often find items as large as muskrat skulls in great horned owl pellets or loose amidst the leaf litter in an area where pellets are found.

If you plan to make a pellet collection, beware that some insects lay their eggs in pellets. When these eggs hatch, your bag of pellets becomes more than you bargained for. We keep our favorite labeled pellets in a container with moth balls.

Hunt for nests

THE EASIEST TIME to find owls is during the breeding season. Not only are they most vocal at this time, but they also keep to a more limited area. Each species breeds at a specific time, and that time varies in different regions. Learn when each of the local owls breeds in your area. Then seri-

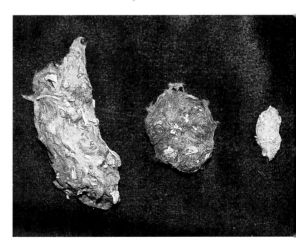

Regurgitated pellets are a tried and true indication that an owl is roosting nearby.

The easiest time to spot owls is in the breeding season. A great gray feeds its young, *above*.

ously begin your search for potential nests so that you are ready when their nesting season begins.

Owls that nest out in the open use plat-formlike nests built by other birds and abandoned after the nesting season. These open-nest owls prefer stick nests built by hawks, crows, ravens, herons and magpies, but a squirrel nest made of twigs and leaves, a clump of witch's broom growth or a viney tangle where leaves have collected may be used if it is all that is available.

Great horned and long-eared owls always use an open nest with a view (as opposed to nesting deep down inside a tree cavity).

Hawk owls, barred owls and spotted owls may also use an open stick nest, but are more commonly found using hollow stumps or cavities inside hollow trees.

Look for open stick nests on edges of open habitat and in pockets of woods away from human disturbance. These nests are commonly high up in a lone evergreen within a woods and are often near water, either a marsh or a wet depression. Not all nests are in pines and other evergreens, though these trees offer some of the best cover. Nests in deciduous trees are often built in the crotch of the tree where several large branches fork.

Do not overlook osprey nests or abandoned eagle nests. Great horned owls frequently use them. They have also been found nesting on man-made deer hunter stands (platforms attached to trees). In the West, where trees are at a premium, look for potential nests on ledges of vertical cliffs. And where cacti predominate, check every stick nest built in branching cacti.

Since the actual nest builders (hawks, crows, ravens and magpies) are active by day, be on the alert for their courtship displays and nest-building activity. If you discover the nest of one of these birds, do not forget about it at the end of the nesting season. Owls may take over the nest the following winter or spring. Keep a diary or a map of all discovered potential owl nests.

Begin your search for owl nest sites as soon as the leaves fall. Explore through the winter, keeping detailed notes in your nest diary of the location and height of each discovered nest. You will be amazed how difficult they sometimes are to find again, especially once deciduous trees develop leaves or if the lighting is different on your return visit. Return to potential nests on a regular basis once the nesting season has begun for the open-nest owls in your area. Look carefully for any signs of use.

All birds need to preen to keep their feathers in the ready for foul weather or for flight in the face of danger. While preening, downy and aged feathers come loose. Sometimes these feathers get caught in the nest edge. Also, as owls take flight from the nest edge, feathers may get caught or fall onto the forest floor. Something as simple as a downy feather hanging on the edge of a stick nest may be the lone giveaway that the nest is in use.

The two owls that always use open nests have ear tufts: great horned and long-eared owls. Incubating and brooding adult owls will crouch way down in the nest. If the nest is large enough, the owl will be all but invisible. But usually, if you look from just the right angle, the spooky but distinct outline of the owl's ear tufts is just visible above the nest rim.

We once circled completely around a seemingly small nest looking for owl signs without any luck. As we walked away, one last look revealed a female great horned owl glaring back at us.

The telltale ear tufts of a long-eared owl can give away the bird's presence on its nest.

Quite a few small owls, such as elf owls, nest in cavities in cacti and hollow trees.

The owl was only visible from one spot, and completely hidden from view from all other angles.

Other telltale signs of an active nest might be a male owl on vigil nearby being harassed by crows, or discarded egg shells lying on the ground, which have been tossed out of the nest by the adult once the young are hatched (although they are usually carried some distance away from the nest to deter predators).

Quite a few of the smaller owls are "hole nesters" and seek natural tree cavities in hollow trees, tree limbs or abandoned holes drilled by woodpeckers in trees, fence posts, telephone or utility poles, cacti and mesquites. They may even use man-made nest boxes built specifically for owls, woodpeckers or wood ducks. Boreal, saw-whet, screech, pygmy and elf owls always use hole nests.

As you are driving, look into the passing landscape for potential nest holes and stick nests. Explore likely habitat on foot or by bike, and always be on the lookout for cavities. It's much harder to determine if an owl is using a particular hole than to verify its use of an open nest.

There are ways to check, however, that are much safer than climbing up to the

Tapping or scratching on a nest tree will sometimes draw the owl into the entrance hole.

are mobbing a hole or an actual owl. Songbirds flying at the entrance to a hole is another excellent clue that an owl may be in residence. Sometimes, "pishing" (repeating "pish-pish") while near a hole will trigger songbirds to come in and mob the hole. This clue should be followed up carefully. Keep a record of holes that have been mobbed by songbirds and return cautiously to them regularly in hopes of finding the owl sunning in the entrance or the entire family out sunning on a nearby branch.

Take a more active approach when searching for hole nesters: Tap or scratch on trees, poles or cacti with holes in them. This sometimes draws the owl out to the hole entrance. This technique seems to work particularly well with saw-whet owls, yet poorly with screech owls. In our years of tapping and scratching on tree trunks with good-looking holes, we've never had an owl look out at us, but we have heard too many stories from those who have had luck to stop now.

hole, especially if the tree is hollow or dead. (Besides the danger involved in scaling a dead tree, climbing to the hole may result in unduly alarming the owl and driving it away.) On cold, sunny winter days or following damp, chilly weather, an owl will sometimes sit in the entrance to the hole to warm itself in the sun.

Be alert for agitated songbirds. If you hear them, approach slowly and quietly, and look through your binoculars to see if they

Short-eared and snowy owls nest right on the ground. Short-eareds nest on salt marshes and freshwater marshes and in tall-grass meadows and agricultural lands. Sometimes their nests are destroyed when a fallow field is plowed. Snowy owls nest north of the tree line in the Arctic directly on the barren ground of the tundra. Burrowing owls, true to their name, nest underground in abandoned burrows originally dug by prairie dogs, ground squirrels, foxes, badgers or armadillos.

The barn owl is one of the most adaptable owls. They use any number of situations as nest sites as long as they are fairly secluded and near good feeding habitat. They will nest in tree cavities; on ledges in barns, abandoned buildings or silos; in church steeples; in rock outcrops, caves, mines or burrows in river banks; on girders under bridges; in man-made nest boxes; and in duck blinds.

The breeding season is a very vulnerable time for owls. Excess disturbance directly affects their breeding success. Owls will use the same nest site year after year if they feel it is safe and if it is not destroyed by weather or the activity of their own young.

All this is fair warning to the owl seeker. If you are fortunate enough to locate an owl nest, study it from afar with binoculars or a telescope. Do not unduly disturb a nest for any reason, including to take a pho-

Burrowing owls, *top*, nest underground, often in abandoned prairie dog burrows. Highly adaptable barn owls, *bottom*, use tree cavities, caves and buildings.

tograph. An adult owl will attack potential predators, and that means you if you are too close to its nest. The famous bird photographer Eric Hosking lost an eye to a tawny owl during a photo session when he was climbing to a blind near its nest.

Excessive activity near an owl's nest may result in nest failure by keeping the adults away from the nest for too long a period. It may also lead predators to the nest, or it may alarm the young to the point that one might fall from the nest. Also, resist the urge to show an active nest to your friends. They may bring their friends, whom you have no control over at all, and nest visits and disturbance will greatly increase. By maintaining proper nest etiquette you will ensure your own future owl study.

Owls during daylight

MOST OWLS ARE NOCTURNAL; only hawk owls and pygmy owls are truly diurnal. But a few owls are crepuscular (active during the dim hours of dawn and dusk or on overcast days). These include snowy owls, short-eared owls, burrowing owls, great gray owls and great horned owls to a lesser degree. The diurnal and crepuscular owls offer rare opportunities to study owls: their behavior, hunting techniques, flight and unique shape. If any of these owls inhabit your area, either as breeders or wintering birds, go out of your way to observe them as frequently as possible. What you learn from diurnal and crepuscular owls will add immensely to your knowledge and understanding of all owls.

Birding hotlines will alert you to the arrival of wintering diurnal and crepuscular owls in your area. If some of these owls do not regularly reach your area, consider embarking on a birding trip if one shows up within a reasonable distance. If you check in periodically with birding hotlines, you may not have to travel as far as you might think.

We have made an annual winter pilgrimage from our New Jersey home to New England to spot snowy owls and have spent hours studying them. Try to locate them during the day and then return in the early evening to watch the show begin. There is nothing quite so special as observing the transformation of an owl as dusk draws near and the hunt begins.

During the day the owl is mostly inactive. The head turns as activity occurs around the bird, but it looks sleepy and seems to be moving in slow motion. At dusk, the hunt begins and the bird immediately moves to a perch with a commanding view. The snowy owl's yellow eyes open wide and the head begins to snap this way and that on an otherwise immobile body.

You know the victim has been selected when the owl's head begins to bob up and down and move from side to side as the owl triangulates on the prey's exact location. Sometimes it loses interest—perhaps the sound of its prey is lost as the wind whooshes through the grasses. At other times, the owl becomes more and more active—it moves its weight back and forth

Often seen south of their Arctic range in winter, snowy owls feed at dusk and dawn.

A snowy owl stays low to the ground as it flies toward its unsuspecting prey.

from one feathered foot to the other.

Don't take your eyes off the owl, even for an instant, or you will miss the hunt. The owl leaves its perch suddenly and flies directly toward its prey on bowed wings, flapping only occasionally and flying so low that it sometimes disappears behind grasses or down into creek bottoms. At the last possible moment, it lifts up slightly only to pounce down on the prey. The meal is swallowed whole in one or two gulps, and almost immediately the owl takes its place on the original perch or a new hunting perch with another commanding view.

This priceless learning period will come to an end all too quickly as it becomes too dark to see. Many of the nocturnal owls also hunt in this manner but we will rarely, if ever, have an opportunity to study them. If, with the aid of moonlight or snow cover, you can see one of the nocturnal owls hunting, it will mean much more to you having studied a snowy owl in action.

Take time to drink in that distinctive owl shape as you study a perched snowy owl: the bulky, headless form with no apparent neck separating the head from the body. Having studied a snowy owl or any of the crepuscular owls, you will find yourself much more prepared to make a positive identification (hawk or owl) when you see a perched raptor silhouette.

Short-eared owls are not easy to locate during the day. They perch communally on the ground hidden in tall grasses or, if there is deep snow cover, in dense evergreens. At that magic moment when dimming light triggers the beginning of their "day," one or several may suddenly appear.

Short-eareds often hunt in flight, crisscrossing low over fields, meadows or marsh. It is quite an education to watch one hunt near enough that you can see the head turning from side to side as the bird's facial disc reflects sound to its ears. Their flight is low and buoyant over the grasses and almost seems to be an attempt to flush prey from the tall vegetation.

Occasionally, a short-eared owl will land on a perch with a commanding view. The body remains stationary, but the head snaps this way and that as the bird directs its eyes for a better look and its facial disc for a better "listen." Again, do not look away. Flight is sudden and direct as the owl heads for its next meal. At the last moment, it flares up and then drops down head first on its prey.

Since short-eared owls are communal in winter, there is a good chance you will have an opportunity to study more than one at a time. If they've found good hunting grounds, short-eareds tend to remain for most of the winter and will give you a priceless, winter-long opportunity to study owls in flight. You will be immediately struck by their unique appearance: a tubular shape with long, wide wings. Each wing beat is stiff as the wings move above and below the body. This gives most owls a buoyant look and is one reason their flight has been described as mothlike. Flapping is interspersed with long glides. Short-eared owls and most other owls glide on bowed wings. Their wide wings droop down in the sailing

Short-eared owls hide during the day in tall grasses, making them hard to locate.

position between periods of flapping.

When short-eared owls first begin to hunt at dusk, northern harriers are just finishing their day. For a brief period, both hunt in the same habitat. Short-eared owls are quite feisty and interact regularly with each other and with nearby northern harriers. You may first be alerted to this by their barking yaplike calls as one tangles in the air with the other.

Because short-eared-owl and northern-harrier periods of activity overlap, you also have a rare opportunity to compare the flap and glide of an owl with that of a hawk. Hawks, in contrast to owls, glide on flat or slightly raised wings. A harrier's flap is firm and the flight more steady than that of the bounding, swerving short-eared owl.

Another lesson to be learned from short-eareds, which is true of many owls, is their attraction to edges where one habitat meets another. Edges attract the greatest variety of creatures and so offer some of the best feeding habitat to a predator. On that moonlit night when you next try to spot one of the nocturnal owls, direct your attention to places where the woods meet the marsh or meadow, or where high marsh meets low marsh, or where creek or river meets upland. Your quest may be more successful.

Burrowing owls might be found by day perched somewhere near their burrow, but they are normally quite inactive during daylight hours. Toward dusk, however, they come alive and fly to a suitable perch with a good view. Their head swivels on an otherwise immobile body as they listen for potential prey. This up-and-down, side-to-side head bobbing gets very vigorous just before they take off toward their detected prey.

Like so many of the owls, burrowing owls depend mostly on hearing to locate their prey. It is fascinating to watch a burrowing owl or a snowy owl hunt and realize that their detection of prey is sometimes totally aural rather than visual.

The hawk owl is probably the truest diurnal owl. The few that we have seen put on incredible performances all day long. Look for them on high perches with commanding views. One we studied in coastal Maine preferred the top of utility poles along a country road. Like other owls, hawk owls depend greatly on their hearing and turn their facial discs back and forth to locate potential prey.

We watched one hawk owl hunt with two feet of snow cover. The bird detected prey 50 feet away and under the snow. It did the same head bobbing and weaving that we had watched other owls do to triangulate on their prey, then flew directly toward one spot. At the last minute, it flared up and pounced down in the snow, mashing its body up and down to pin the prey. Then, its entire head and bill penetrated the snow and miraculously came up with a rodent. We had previously had the opportunity to see this from afar and in poor light, but not until this encounter did we realize how much of a role owls' exceptional hearing plays in successful hunting.

Northern hawk owls are one of the few owl species that hunt during daylight.

Following Up Clues

SLEUTHING FOR OWLS will be far more productive once you recognize certain clues and follow them up. Some clues like songbirds "scolding" or crows "mobbing" often indicate the presence of an owl (or other predators, like snakes or hawks) and should be followed up immediately. Other clues are less direct but just as important, like the discovery of road-killed owls or daytime observations of certain hawks that have a nighttime owl counter-part. Following up these less direct clues often means taking detailed notes of dates and sites on an accurate map, followed by methodical and repeated visits to each site. Recognizing clues and following them up will make you a successful owl seeker.

Grassy shoulders make roadsides attractive to both rodents and owls. *Above*, a saw-whet.

Road-killed owls

ONCE YOU BEGIN looking for them, road-killed owls are, sadly, found with some frequency. A dead owl on a roadside should never be ignored. Check its legs for a U.S. Fish and Wildlife Service band. If the bird is banded, record the band number, the date found, the exact location, the condition of the bird, the cause of death and the type of owl if known. Then send the information to: Department of the Interior, Bird Banding Laboratory, Office of Migratory Bird Management, Patuxent Wildlife Research Center, Laurel, MD 20708. Banded or not, report your finding to your local bird club or Audubon group. Even a dead owl is significant and,

An owl's habit of flying low makes it vulnerable to road-kill. *Above*, a long-eared owl.

depending on when you find it, adds to an understanding of the owl's dispersal, winter range or breeding territory.

Nature centers, universities and museums have the proper permits to hold dead birds and are always grateful to receive road-killed specimens, if not too damaged, for future use for educational purposes. This is the case with the Cape May Bird Observatory, and over the course of one winter (1988-89), 37 road-killed saw-whet owls were reported to us. They had been found in South Jersey along the Garden State Parkway and a few other major roads near the Atlantic Coast. Piecing the picture together, we realized that there were proba-

bly hundreds of saw-whet owls wintering in South Jersey that year, far more than usual.

Roadsides with wide, grassy shoulders often have a healthy population of rodents and rabbits. Since all predators are opportunistic, roads with these conditions will undoubtedly attract hawks by day and owls by night. You have probably noticed red-tailed hawks perched in trees right next to thruways, interstates and other major roads with these conditions. Unfortunately, road kills are inevitable, especially with owls, since many of them hunt low to the ground.

This low flight may help the owl surprise its prey, and it may be necessary because of the owl's dependence on hearing. Perhaps

The presence of red-tailed hawks, *top*, in an area by day indicates that great horned owls, *bottom*, may hunt the same area at night.

all too often takes owls right into the path of moving cars. Collisions with vehicles are a major cause of mortality in some owl species.

Road-killed owls can help the owl spotter locate roosts, so keep a record of road-kills—noting the location and date found. Owl mystic Ed Manners ventures into the woods' edge whenever he finds a road-killed saw-whet to find the bird's daytime roost. Having studied a very successful winter saw-whet owl roost since 1961 that attracts between 10 and 20 birds (with the highest winter count of 57 birds), he knows what he is looking for.

More than once, when Ed returned to a road-killed owl's roost a week later or sometimes even sooner, he found a new saw-whet owl using the same perch. On one occasion, the second saw-whet was also hit by a car, and less than a week later, a third bird moved into the roost, using the very same branch the other two had used.

There is no harm in taking a closer look at a road-killed owl in good condition. First study the serrated leading edge to each primary feather on the wing, which looks as if it has been thinned with scissors. (In most other birds, the primary feathers along the leading edge of the wing have a hard, crisp edge, which causes a whooshing sound as they fly.) This softened leading edge makes for silent flight: as the wing moves through the air, this edge creates little resistance and therefore no sound. Also

during its entire flight, the owl uses its hearing to track the potential prey's movements up until the moment of capture. Unfortunately, low flight, in the proximity of roads, notice how every feather on an owl is covered with a soft furriness, which also means less resistance and ensures silent flight.

Carefully study the owl's lethally sharp talons and its face, which is a flattened disc. You can readily see how the shape of an owl's face reflects sound back to the ears, hidden behind the facial disc. Notice too how the eyes are set in front of the head (unlike most other birds' eyes, which are set on either side of the head), enabling an owl to have binocular vision.

Convergent evolution

HAWKS AND OWLS are excellent examples of convergent evolution, where two groups have evolved similar traits even though they came from different ancestors. Hawks and owls have similar structure, plumage patterns and behavior. Some hawks and owls are counterparts of one another. Red-tailed hawks and great horned owls are found in exactly the same habitats and locations. Where you see a red-tailed hawk by day, you may very likely find a great horned owl filling the same niche at night. Since hawks are diurnal, they are more commonly seen and are important clues to the probable presence of certain owls.

The deep, wet woods where you find red-shouldered hawks may be home to barred owls by night. And where you see northern harriers hunting by day, you are likely to find short-eared owls hunting at dusk. Open areas with woodlots and orchards that attract hunting American kestrels by day are often home to screech owls by night. If you should

repeatedly see one of these hawks during the day, go back at dusk and look for its nighttime counterpart.

Owl indicators

OWLS ARE SUCCESSFUL predators. All predators trigger a reaction from other creatures. Some creatures are very vocal in their reaction, especially crows, ravens, jays and chickadees. Songbirds "scolding" or crows "mobbing" should send up an immediate red flag—they've found a predator. Drop everything and head toward the commotion. It might be short-lived. Be as stealthy as possible in your approach, using trees and brush to camouflage your shape as you near the spot. If you approach with caution, your chances are good of seeing just what has caused all the agitation, since the immediate commotion is so distracting to the predator that it is robbed of some of its normal alertness.

When you are near enough to get a view of the birds causing the commotion (but not so close as to disrupt them), stop and scan with binoculars. Focus your attention on the very center of the activity. If the crows keep diving on one particular spot, try to see through the leaves and branches to determine just what they have cornered. Songbirds will sometimes fly at a predator, but more frequently will hop closer and closer to it.

If you are still having a hard time seeing the cause of the commotion, then consider moving closer, but do so very cautiously and slowly. Speaking from experience, we can assure you that one snapped branch is all it takes to flush an owl before you've had a chance to even identify it. A second approach will be much more difficult once the predator is aware of your presence.

After a lengthy and cautious approach and finally a good look, you may find that all the commotion was caused by a snake, a cat or a hawk. But if you have discovered an owl, study it as long as you can. The cornered nocturnal predator caught exposed during the day is highly alert as it glares at its attackers. Study its magnificent camouflage.

If it should flush, remain where you are and follow it with your binoculars. Be ready to see it drop off the branch or slip effortlessly out of the evergreen and glide silently away on bowed wings. Even a quick flush is educational since you will understand why you can so easily miss owls when walking through the forest, and why you must constantly scan ahead.

One of the most camouflaged saw-whet owls we ever found was discovered by chickadees in the center of a honeysuckle tangle right next to a trail. Hundreds of birders had taken the trail that day, since it was the peak of the fall migration at Higbee Beach Wildlife Management Area, near Cape May, New Jersey. But no one had seen the saw-whet until one alert birder curiously observed a group of agitated chickadees. Even today, looking at the photograph we took, we have a hard time seeing the saw-whet owl discreetly perched next to a clump of oak leaves caught in the honeysuckle tangle.

On another occasion, during an overcast Christmas Bird Count, chickadees and titmice reacted to our "pishing" by congregating around a small dead tree. As we circled the tree, we found one side so decayed that a screech owl hidden inside was easily visible. It remained perfectly still, trying not to be seen, and if not for the chickadees we would certainly have missed it.

Chickadees are known for their name-saying call, "chick-a-dee-dee-dee." But when you hear this call repeated over and over again in an agitated manner, hop to it and see what they've discovered. As with any approach toward a possible owl, move in slowly, cautiously and quietly with binoculars at the ready.

Scolding chickadees may indicate the presence of a well-hidden owl, such as this saw-whet.

60

Owling Etiquette

~

1. Never use tapes or imitations during an owl's breeding season unless you are part of a legitimate, organized survey.

2. Never use tapes where they are illegal. This includes all national parks where tapes are considered a form of wildlife harassment.

A natural camouflage of branches and berries obscures this long-eared owl.

3. Never use tapes with threatened or endangered species, unless you are part of a legitimate, organized survey.

4. If you should discover an owl, be very still and quiet and do everything in slow motion.

5. Upon discovery, sink slowly to the ground to appear less threatening. If the owl no longer feels threatened, you may get to watch it relax—a real treat.

6. If you are too close to the owl and it fidgets and continues to look alarmed (elongated), back off very slowly and quietly, keeping your profile low.

7. If you find a nest or roost site and wish to study it, visit infrequently (no more than once every 3 to 4 weeks).

8. Study a nest or roost site from a safe distance with binoculars or a telescope, so the owl is not alarmed by your presence.

9. Do not disturb a nest or roost site by getting too close (even for photos). You may be the reason a nest fails or a roost is abandoned.

10. Do not snap branches away from an owl or its perch for the "perfect photo." Owls choose to perch with branches breaking up their overall shape, a natural camouflage. The branches make the photo realistic.

11. Protect your discovered owl by keeping it a secret; refrain from telling your friends. They may tell their friends, and before you know it, the cumulative disturbance will drive the owl away.

12. Use basic birding etiquette at all times. Respect private property and "no trespassing" signs. Amherst Island, Ontario, that special spot discussed so often in this book, no longer welcomes birders because of numerous infractions of these basics.

Equipment Know-How

OWLING DOES NOT require much overhead; all that is usually needed is energy, stamina and strong legs. Often checking "just one more time" or "just one more grove" will be the key to success. Nevertheless, some basic equipment can be very helpful.

Compass and maps

A GOOD HAND COMPASS and topographic maps (source: Map Distribution,

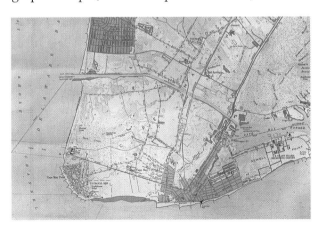

Detailed topographic maps can be particularly useful for guiding owlers into remote areas.

U.S. Geological Survey, Box 25286, Federal Center, Denver, CO 80225) for your area will enable you to stray confidently from the beaten path. Finding owls means finding the proper habitat, and topographic base maps can tell you a lot about new places and even reveal secrets about areas you thought you knew quite well. These maps are particularly helpful in guiding you into remote habitats.

Binoculars

IN ALL ASPECTS of owling, binoculars are indispensable, whether you are looking for an owl shape on a horizon at dusk or hunting through deep woods for owl signs. Owling does require good binoculars. If you are thinking of buying a pair specifically for owling, look for a pair with good twilight capabilities. The lower-power binoculars let in more light and are better in low-light conditions than the higher-power binoculars. Look for 7x (seven-power)

Low-power binoculars with good twilight capabilities are an indispensable owling tool.

binoculars as opposed to 10x or higher-powered binoculars.

Avoid zoom, automatic focus or fixed-focus binoculars. By and large, optics that fall in these categories offer marginal quality and less than marginal performance. We don't know of any serious birders who have stayed with their zoom binoculars over time. And we don't know of any who prefer non-wheel focusing mechanisms, such as rocker focus switches. These are finicky and, for us, detract from the instant, crisp focusing that the old-fashioned focusing wheel gives. In the end, you really cannot beat the old standard 7x42 or 7x50 binoc-

ulars for both owling and general birding.

Telescopes and tripods

THERE CERTAINLY ARE TIMES when you will want more optical power than your binoculars can give. For many owl species, particularly the open country ones (snowy, short-eared and burrowing), you will want to scan distant marshes and grasslands for silhouettes. For this, we recommend a spotting scope. Again, do not try for too high a power. A scope with a power between 20x and 30x is best. Also, be sure your telescope eyepiece is wide-angle.

For best results in low-light conditions, select a telescope with a wide-angle eyepiece.

additional light and function better in low-light conditions. Stay away from zoom eyepieces. Even at low magnification they offer a marginal field of view.

Do not skimp when you purchase a tripod. A cheap, shaky tripod makes the whole setup unusable no matter how good the scope is. We have seen top-of-the-line scopes on cheap tripods and have had far better views through a low-budget scope on a good tripod. Much of your scanning will no doubt be done in windy, wintery conditions, where "scope shake" is a real problem, so a sturdy tripod is a must.

Keep in mind, too, that once you've found your quarry, you will want to enjoy it for as long as you can. If it is bitter cold, you will want to keep your hands in your pockets, protected from the elements, not exposed and holding the tripod in place. A gust of wind can easily blow over and shatter your investment. We prefer the tripods now available with a fluid head. A fluid head makes scanning much easier. Older tripod heads require loosening and tightening all sorts of handles to position the scope on the quarry. If the quarry moved, this meant some fast maneuvering to keep it in view. The fluid head allows you to rotate the scope in any direction you want without loosening and tightening any handles.

Telescope eyepieces are interchangeable. If the telescope you want comes with a certain eyepiece that is not what we've recommended, be sure to order a 20x, 22x or 30x wide-angle eyepiece. The wide-angle capability makes scanning easier because your field of view is wider than with standard eyepieces. Wide-angle eyepieces also let in

For more information on optics, consult birding magazines. *Birding*, published by the American Birding Association (ABA), has published a number of quality reviews, comparison tests and optic evaluations in the last few years. Also check to see if your local nature center offers workshops on optics for birders. Some regularly offer these as a service to help birders and naturalists come to a decision when making a first purchase or when upgrading.

Tape recorders

A TAPE RECORDER is useful, though not essential, to owling. You can play back recorded tapes of owl calls in hopes of eliciting a response from the real thing.

First, you will need a source of owl calls. For this, the *Peterson Field Guides to Bird Songs* (available for the eastern/central birds and the western birds) is a good place to start. Many regional recordings and recordings of specific groups of birds are available as well, by mail order through ABA and often at nature-center bookstores.

In most cases, these recordings may be purchased as records, cassette tapes and compact discs. If you have a CD system, we recommend that you make tapes from CDs. Not only is the CD sound quality the best of all three modes, but you can search for a particular bird song or owl call much more easily on a CD than you can on a record or tape. Also, CD players make the creation of a tape for field use much easier. With an instant backtrack feature, owl calls can be repeated again and again with ease as you lay down a series of calls on your tape.

A wide variety of tape decks are available for field use. For actual owl census efforts,

Windy, open field conditions make "scope shake" a problem, so a sturdy tripod is a must.

we have used an elaborate tape deck designed for harsh field conditions. This has a plug-in loudspeaker to broadcast sound. It is loud, but heavy and bulky. We find that a small, cheap cassette deck, more commonly called a "boom box," will work just fine. The smaller, compact models are easily carried by their handle or will fit in a backpack. The waterproof models are ideal.

We use a double-deck model, which holds two tapes, so we can call for two species of owls in quick succession without fumbling with a flashlight to change tapes. Memorize the button positions so that you can operate the deck in the dark without using a flashlight, which will ruin your night vision. Place masking tape over the "record" button so you can't push it accidentally and ruin your tape.

Some people use pocket tape recorders, and these seem to be perfectly appropriate. They are far more compact and easier to carry and operate than even the smallest boom boxes available, but they may not project the recording as far.

Tape loudness, however, is not all that critical to success. Remember how good an owl's hearing is. We usually play tapes at a low volume. When an owl finally does respond, you may be fooled about how close it is. We have found screech and saw-whet owls that we thought were about 100 yards away in a tree right next to us, only 20 feet away.

You can place a number of owl calls on the same tape, but then you must constantly rewind and fast-forward while in the field. We prefer to use loop tapes, such as those designed for answering machines. We carry separate tapes, one for saw-whet owls, one for barred owls, etc. Simply change the tape to survey for a different species. Use the 60-second loop tape. Record one or two call sequences on the tape and leave the rest blank. When in the field, let it play continuously for three to five minutes, then listen for three to five minutes. Remember, most owls do not call nonstop (except saw-whet and pygmy owls), and you need some listening time built in too.

Flashlights

A GOOD FLASHLIGHT is one of the most important tools when owl spotting. We prefer either a good quality "mag-lite" or a six-volt hand-held lantern. The newer models advertising halogen bulbs are by far the brightest and the best.

But do not use the very bright 300,000 or 1,000,000 candlepower 12-volt lights on owls. Although we do know people who use them, we simply cannot believe these do not temporarily impair an owl's vision. We have looked into these searchlights and our night vision has been nonexistent for 15 minutes. An owl's vision is far more acute and sensitive than ours. Even if the owl does recover soon, we do not wish to be the cause of a saw-whet owl being picked off by a great horned owl because its vision was temporarily impaired by an overeager owl seeker.

Once you have located the bird, do not shine your light directly on it; hold the light slightly off-center. This way, the bird will probably stay put longer. Repeated direct beams will sometimes flush the bird.

Night-vision aids

A FEW OF US have tried watching owls during their time—at night, using night-vision binoculars and scopes. In 1982, Clay and Pete Dunne, then-director of New Jersey Audubon Society's Cape May Bird Observatory, hatched a project to study the nocturnal owl migration at Cape May. Using surplus night scopes on loan from the U.S. Army, we attempted to actually count owls migrating past the Cape May Point Lighthouse.

Occasionally used by researchers, night-vision aids are not necessary for the recreational owler.

The project was less than satisfying, although marginally successful from a scientific standpoint. The scopes were heavy, awkward, only 3x and caused extreme, almost debilitating, eye fatigue. They were designed for the military, not birders. They were hard to scan with, but, if you did find an owl, you really could watch it at night. Researcher Bob Russell and others recorded 210 owls that fall, in 178 hours of observation. Saw-whets were seen skimming the marsh, barn owls circling high overhead and long-eared owls leaving the trees after dark, continuing on their journey south.

It was a good idea, theoretically, but we can hardly recommend these ancient night-vision scopes to anyone. Recently, however, the exigencies of military research have made great strides in artificial night vision. Today, light-enhancement and infrared night binoculars, scopes and even helmets with built-in night binoculars have been greatly improved.

Lately we have noted second- and third-generation night-vision binoculars and scopes being offered for sale in police/military, boating and sporting-goods catalogs. We know little of their quality or performance, but we suspect that military state-of-the-art night-vision equipment could contribute greatly to owl study. Unfortunately, we do not know if those currently available to the public will do the necessary job, and even so, they are extremely expensive—probably more than the average weekend owl watcher wishes to pay.

Backyard Owling

IF YOU WANT TO FIND and see owls, start in your own backyard. It is not such a far-fetched idea. Screech owls are quite suited to both rural and suburban settings, and sometimes are even found in city parks. Barn owls will nest in barns, silos or abandoned outbuildings if they can get in and out when they please and if they can find enough to eat in the surrounding fields and meadows. They can sometimes be found in towns and cities as well. Great horned owls are remarkably adaptable, and are found over all of North America.

An owl may be attracted to your property if you manage it for wildlife or, as some people say, "fail to manage it." Owls, like other birds, will be more attracted to your yard if you encourage a more natural look and tolerate weedy edges and tangles. A highly manicured, rich green lawn of monoculture growth, where weeds are not tolerated, is not much more than a green desert to wildlife.

Since owls are predators, they need prey, so your yard must be attractive to other wildlife for owls to be attracted to it. Begin by working on a backyard habitat plan for your property. Make your yard hospitable to wildlife by leaving some cover and providing plenty of natural foods by planting a variety of native trees and shrubs, including evergreens.

Evergreens and tangles of vines like honeysuckle and grape are just the sort of places that owls and other birds use as roost sites in the wild. Leave hollow trees standing

Barn owls, *above*, nest in human structures and sometimes venture into urban areas. *Left*, screech owls are extremely adaptable.

A backyard that is attractive to other kinds of wildlife will inevitably draw in nearby owls.

and don't cut off hollow limbs—these are ready-made nest sites for hole-nesting owls and other birds and animals, and they may be used at other times of the year for roost sites and as a shelter from bad weather.

If you do not already have a hollow tree, erect a nest box suited to owls that may live in your area. The easiest hole-nesting owl to attract to a suburban setting is the screech owl. The standard nest box for screech owls, with its 3-inch entrance hole, is also suitable for American kestrels.

If your property or the adjoining area has wet, wooded swamps or woodlands, you might attract a barred owl with your efforts or you may already have one nesting if you have hollow trees standing. They, too, may be attracted to a man-made nest box. The saw-whet owl is another hole nester to look for in northern regions. It will readily use a screech owl nest box, but the entrance hole needs to be smaller: 2½ inches.

If you are lucky enough to live where boreal owls might be found, try putting up a screech owl box to attract them, but make the entrance hole larger: 3½ inches. We are not sure if anyone has ever had luck with nest boxes for elf owls or pygmy owls, but it won't hurt to try if the habitat is available and nest sites are scarce.

Resident and migratory owls might be attracted to your yard if you have active bird-feeding stations and nearby evergreen plantings. During the day, birds attracted to the feeders scatter seed onto the ground. This attracts rodents by night, which in turn attracts rodent predators, such as owls.

At Cape May each fall, when hundreds of saw-whet owls migrate through, we nearly always learn of someone who has had one of these tiny owls perch for a night or two or even part of the winter in an evergreen, either a red cedar or a holly tree, near a bird feeder. The evergreen situated near the feeder provides a safe place for the owl to spend the day while scoping for prey.

If you have had some success in your own backyard, why not turn your energy to your community. All open spaces, like parks, ball fields and even railroad and power line right-of-ways, are potential wildlife habitats. Introduce the concept of wildlife plantings and provide nest boxes. The more extensive the suitable habitat, the better your chances are of attracting owls and holding them.

Barn owls have become quite rare in some parts of the country, even where farming persists, because of today's intensive farming practices. The historic reduction of wetland habitats, the loss of farm acreage to urban sprawl and the move away from pastures, hayfields and meadows to more intensive row-crop farming over the past 40 years has put the barn owl on the endangered species list in seven Midwestern states (Illinois, Indiana, Iowa, Michigan, Missouri, Ohio and Wisconsin).

The federal farm bill of 1985 offers incentives to farmers who take land out of crop production and set it aside for conservation purposes. This is critical to barn owl survival in some parts of the country where feeding habitat has become as rare as the owls themselves.

If you suspect barn owls still exist in your area, talk to farmers located near grassland and marsh habitats. Explain the value of pastures, weedy areas and wet meadows. Also point out that each barn owl eats about three mice a day, or about 1,000 mice a year. Thus, one pair of barn owls and their five or

Natural cavity nesters, screech owls are one of the easiest species to attract to man-made nest boxes.

so young would help to limit the rodent population.

Work with the farmers to encourage nesting barn owls by erecting nest boxes in barns, silos and other outbuildings to provide secure nest sites. Something as simple as a 6-inch-square entrance hole (leading to a secure nest box) cut in the wall of a barn might ensure successful nesting. Some nest sites that barn owls attempt to use are not necessarily safe. For example, hollow tree nest sites are subject to collapse or being cut down for firewood. Nests on ledges in barns and silos are insecure: the young can fall from the nest, there can be too much activity so the owls abandon the site, or people may force them out.

Those who live within the northern range of boreal owls, _left_, can attract them to nest boxes. _Above_, holes cut in a barn's siding admit barn owls.

Plans for barn owl nest boxes are available from The Barn Owl Research Foundation (P.O. Box 680183, San Antonio, TX 78238); this nonprofit organization is responsible for the most intensive adult barn owl population study in the world (conducted in southwestern New Jersey). While you have the farmer's cooperation, get permission to put up screech owl/American kestrel nest boxes (the same box serves both species) on the wooded edges of the fields.

This accumulation of owl-finding hints and thoughts grew from our years of seeking, observing, studying and appreciating owls and the mysteries of the outdoors. May this book gently guide you to discoveries of your own. Once you have read the species accounts you will be ready to go out and spot some owls on your own. Good luck! And remember, you never seem to see or find what you are looking for, but quite often you discover something just as interesting and exciting. And you certainly won't ever find what you are looking for if you don't go out and look. Enjoy owling for what it is, a wonderful excuse to be outdoors!

If you become an owl addict like us, you may be able to channel your interest in owls into a rewarding research project. On an annual (sometimes semiannual) basis _Winging It_, ABA's newsletter, includes a "Directory of Volunteer Opportunities for Birders"—a thorough listing of volunteer job opportunities state by state with the U.S. Forest Service, the U.S. Bureau of Land Management, the U.S. National Park Service, the U.S. Fish and Wildlife Service and the Canadian Wildlife Service. Many of these opportunities are ongoing and many involve owls or raptors in general.

Part Two:
The Owls of North America

Owls You Can Spot

Great Horned Owl

Bubo virginianus
Length: 21"
Wingspan: 45"

The great horned owl, found from the high Arctic tree line to the arid canyons of the southwest and from the barrier beach islands of the Atlantic Coast to the cliffs at Point Reyes on the Pacific Coast, is the most widespread North American owl species. It is found throughout South America as well, from the Andes to Tierra Del Fuego, and from the Llanos to the rain forest. It is also the most abundant owl throughout much of North America.

With its huge talons, the great horned is one of North America's most powerful birds of prey. It has the most varied diet of any of the owls, eating anything from cray-fish to young fox. These owls favor rabbits, rats, mice and birds (even other smaller owls). During the fall migration at Cape May, we once found a saw-whet owl skull inside a great horned's pellet.

Great horneds will also eat snakes, frogs, fish, muskrats, skunks and many other species of prey, including feral kittens. In the northeast, there are numerous records of great horned owls feeding on both adult and juvenile red-shouldered hawks. Maurice Broun, Hawk Mountain Sanctuary's first curator, once saw a great horned catch and kill a red-tailed hawk as it migrated past the lookout on the mountain.

The great horned owl, along with the bald eagle, is the earliest nesting bird in the United States. By early September, great horned owls are already courting in much of the northeast. At dusk or in the early hours of dawn, you may hear the female answering the male with her low hoots. In October and November, courtship quick-

The great horned owl, *right*, is a formidable predator. *Previous pages*: A saw-whet owl.

ens and by early winter the adults have set up their territory, driving off even their own young from the previous season.

As the time draws near to lay eggs, the great horned owl, also known as the "hoot owl," becomes very vocal. Night after night, and sometimes even during the day, the male and female call to one another. The owls quiet down during the month-long incubation period, when you can be fooled into thinking that they've moved elsewhere.

Each area has its own timetable, so use and adjust the following information to help you determine when to look for great horneds in your area. In New Jersey and Pennsylvania, eggs are laid in late January or early February, and progressively later farther north. Snow may still cover the ground, and winter storms may blanket the female with snow as she remains on the nest, incubating the eggs.

The owlets hatch just as crocuses are beginning to bloom, in late February to early March. Most other bird species are still on their wintering grounds, some are just beginning to migrate north, but all are a good two months away from nesting.

By mid-April the young are still covered with white downy feathers but are so large—nearly the size of the adult—that they are quite obvious in the nest. The nest becomes too confining at this time, and older young may leave it and move onto the surrounding branches. Flight feathers have not yet grown in so the owls can't fly off.

By late April they begin to "branch"—although they cannot yet fly, they begin to hop from branch to branch. As a result, they get harder and harder to find. As soon as the young can fly, they move deeper into the forest to join the adults. The one remaining clue to their presence is their raspy food-begging call at sunset. Listen for this call right through the summer and fall.

For their nest site, great horned owls often choose a stick nest built in a previous year by a hawk, crow, raven or heron. Occasionally in the East these owls will use the hollowed out top of a tree stump, but this is more commonly seen in the West. Throughout the East, a red-tailed hawk's nest will most often be used. Red-tailed hawks build large stick nests high in a pine, in the crotch of a large deciduous tree or on a cliff ledge; out

By late spring, down-covered juvenile great horned owls have grown nearly as large as their parents.

west, where trees are scarce, they may use a utility pole or a saguaro cactus.

Red-tailed hawks will not begin their courtship until a full month after great horned owls have begun to nest, and so will be forced to build and use a new nest somewhere nearby, perhaps only to have the new nest usurped by great horneds the following season. By the time great horned owlets fledge, they have usually destroyed the stick nest they were born in—trampling and breaking it down until, twig by twig, it has fallen to the ground.

Because great horned owls are common and year-round residents, they are relatively easy to find, especially during the nesting season when mated pairs hoot back and forth. Often the female will call from the nest—a valuable clue. If found, a nest should be studied from afar, using a telescope or binoculars. Be sure to view an exposed roadside nest from your car, using it as a blind. A roadside nest or a great horned in an osprey nest on the open marsh will offer an unparalleled opportunity to study the adults and nestlings from a safe distance with a spotting scope.

Because great horned owls are so vocal, there is no reason to resort to tapes to lure them in. In most areas, great horneds call during almost any quiet dawn or dusk, so taping is just disruptive to territorial birds. Also, since the great horned owl's talons are the largest of any North American bird of prey (except eagles), you may not want them to think you are an interloper in their terri-

A great horned owl adopts a defensive position. It is best not to approach owls this closely.

tory! Researchers and photographers have been attacked, usually while climbing to nests, so with great horneds it is best to watch from afar and leave the tapes at home.

Great horned owls should be the novice's first quarry—they are widespread, numerous, very large and easy to hear. Listen to tapes at home to familiarize yourself with their calls. Many beginners have mistaken the cooing of a morning dove for an owl. Also, be aware that young great horned owls have a variety of loud, raucous food-begging calls, and many a confusing noise in the night can be pegged to hungry fledglings.

Great horned owls, like many other owls, often come out to edges overlooking a good feeding habitat at dusk. After the sun has set and during that magical period before full dark, you will not only often hear great horneds, but if you are positioned in the right spot, you will see them come out to perch—along the edges of fields, lakes, marshes and forest clearings. Scan bare snags silhouetted against the dimming light. Patience will be rewarded by the unmistakable eared profile of the great horned owl watching and listening for its prey from its excellent vantage point.

Barred Owl

Strix varia
Length: 20"
Wingspan: 44"

The barred owl, although not as widely distributed as the great horned owl, can be found throughout much of North America. It is at home in the Canadian Rockies, across the dense coniferous forests and wet deciduous woods in the Northeast and in river bottomlands in the Midwest. The greatest population density of barred owls is, however, in the south, where they are common from eastern Texas to the Carolinas and Florida. Here they are found in cypress swamps and in hammocks of mixed palmettos and live oaks, usually near water.

While shy, secretive and easily flushed in the North, the barred owls of the South can be downright tame, and many people's first owl sighting has been of the confiding and cooperative barred owl in places like Corkscrew Swamp, the Everglades National Park or in many of Florida's wonderful state parks.

Since they are less powerful than the great-horned, their diet is not quite as varied. While mice are a mainstay, reptiles and amphibians are preferred when in season.

Barred owls also thrive deep within New Jersey's remaining sizable freshwater wetlands, such as Great Cedar Swamp, Bear Swamp, Manahawkin Swamp, Great Swamp and the Pequannock Watershed. One descends into these lowland forests on old logging trails, traveling farther and farther away from the sights and sounds of people.

Near barred owl haunts, the ground underfoot becomes soggy and moss-covered. Glimpses into the forest reveal large forms—knurled trees with outstretched limbs reach in all directions. These limbs alone are larger than most trees found outside the swamps. Often a sizable hole and a hollow sound to the trunk indicate that the inner core is rotting away. Yet the tree still lives, sending its lifeblood up the outer shell, and perhaps houses that wonderful swamp dweller, the barred owl.

One warm day in March, Pat went seeking barred owls in Great Cedar Swamp. The deciduous trees around her were still leafless. She had come to a stream that was cold, deep and sluggish, like most of Great Cedar Swamp's streams. She began by softly imitating the hoot of a barred owl, "Who cooks for you, who cooks for you all?" and ended it with a string of raucous

Secretive and easily flushed in the North, barred owls can be downright tame in the South.

"owl laughter." The swamp answered in silence, but our dog, baffled by this hooting, began barking at Pat, although she'd accompanied her countless times before in various lesser swamps while censusing owls. As Pat bent to comfort the dog she felt, rather than heard, the silent landing of a barred owl in the tree directly overhead. The owl rotated its large earless head around, seeking with its coal-black eyes the intruder into its inner domain.

March is the beginning of their nesting season and territoriality is strong. Pat's presence did not seem to disturb the barred owl, leading her to wonder if it had ever seen a human before. Pat and the owl talked back and forth a few times, her attempt sounding pitiful in comparison to the eerie and resounding hooting of the owl. Then the owl withdrew just as silently as it had come.

Throughout much of their range, barred owls are less numerous than great horneds, and this, coupled with the fact that they are an owl of dense woodlands, makes them considerably harder to find and watch. They prefer cavities for nesting—a deep hollow in a standing tree—and it is a lucky person who has found a barred owl on a stick nest. Once in a while, they do usurp a hawk or crow nest for their own, however.

Since most nests are invisible deep within a hollow tree, finding one is a bit of a needle in a haystack. Years of tapping on hollow trees during the late spring nesting season has only once yielded a barred owl for us, when a bird flushed from a dead sweet gum tree cavity. There was a clue, however: nesting material hung out of the hole. Probably originally placed there by squirrels, it may have been kicked out of the hole by active young owls. Another time, we saw a large downy feather caught on the edge of a hole, clear evidence that an owl had been present.

Barred owls are best located by voice, but this technique will not be effective year-round since they are not as vocal as great horned owls. During the height of the breeding season, with eggs and young in the nest, they may be quite silent. Only at the onset of breeding (November and December in Florida, February and March in New Jersey and April in New England) are they fairly vocal.

Barred owls call at any hour of the night or day. They are more likely to call after sunrise than predawn, and as apt to call in late afternoon as at full dusk. One bird in New Jersey, in a riparian woodland near a town, always called in reply to the noontime fire whistle!

Because of their strict nocturnal

Barred owls usually raise their young in cavities, but will, on occasion, use a stick nest.

habits and preferred deep-woods habitat, barred owls are often seen only through active luring. In the East, barred owls are very responsive to tapes. If you have trouble finding barred owls by passively listening for them in their preferred lowland habitat, play a tape of their call at dawn or dusk (though not during the breeding season). Play about one minute of calls, followed by one minute of silence, for five to ten minutes. Then, most importantly, wait another ten minutes in silence. Once, while conducting a barred owl survey, which required us to tape for ten minutes then move one-half mile to the next spot, we repeatedly heard barred owls calling from the spot we had just left!

Barred owls prefer deep woods habitats and are usually seen only through active luring at night.

Also, be visually alert. Barred owls will often fly in silently and sit and watch, without calling, as you play the tape. For this reason, taping works better in winter than in summer, when dense foliage may conceal their appearance. At other times, a chorus of barred owls may respond with a cacophony of calling that sounds quite unlike the standard "Who cooks for you?"

One of our greatest loves is to camp among barred owls and have the dreamy pleasure of being awakened by them. We have spent some of our best nights in Francis Marion National Forest in South Carolina, Stephen F. Austin State Park in Texas and Lake Kissimmee State Park in Florida being serenaded by the resounding "Who cooks for you, who cooks for you all?" calls of the barred owl.

Spotted Owl

Strix occidentalis
Length: 18"
Wingspan: 43"

The information was not on the hotline, but Rich Stallcup, an author and bird tour guide from Point Reyes, California, assured us he could lead us to a pair of spotted owls that he had been keeping tabs on. After working the thickly wooded National Forest canyons for over six hours, Rich's enthusiasm had not dampened, but he was scratching his head. "They were here last week, right in this grove, but maybe they've gone over to the next canyon for a while."

Because it is officially listed as an endangered species, the spotted owl should never be harassed.

gave us directions to a ridge trail and sent us off.

The next day we were at the trailhead, ready for our last try for spotted owls before flying back East. We hiked through the old-growth forest until after 3:00 p.m., seeing little in the way of birds, yet drinking in the rich color and grandeur of the big trees. Turning back, we passed two birders who were also in pursuit of the owls. Pleasantries exchanged, we turned toward our car, the airport, New Jersey and home.

Just ten minutes later we heard heavy footfalls coming up fast from behind. "We've found the owls! We hoped we could catch up to you before it was too late." We reversed our direction and followed our new friends back up the path. There, on the moss- and fern-covered branches of an ancient tree, sat a spotted owl. Just 20 feet away sat a downy-covered young spotted owl.

Sitting quietly and speaking in whispered tones, we watched the owls until dusk began to fall. We reluctantly headed back down the trail, leaving only to avoid having to travel the trail in full darkness. As we left, the young bird was becoming active, giving a food-begging call to its mother who was becoming ever more alert as darkness fell.

We were happy and awed just to have seen spotted-owl habitat, but retained a ray of hope when Rich mentioned there was a pair of spotted owls that had been sighted regularly last year over in the next county. He

The story above contains many lessons for owl finders. Talk to local birders. Ask where owls have been sighted. We have relied on several sources of information when traveling. The National Audubon Society Christmas Bird Count issues give names and addresses of count compilers. Check published count results to find high-count locations for those species you are most interested in. Call the local compilers for tips on owl finding. In most cases, they will be very helpful (although it is best to write ahead first).

Today, many good birding areas are thoroughly covered with up-to-date information, maps and directions in the various regional or state birder's guides available for sale through the American Birding Association (ABA) and at some nature centers and bird bookstores. Also check the *Guide to North American Bird Clubs* by J. E. Rickert (1978), and try to attend some club meetings when traveling. Showing this interest will almost always elicit information about the latest sightings. When in the field, talk to other birders and ask for specific directions. Always carry a note pad and be prepared to copy down exact directions. We know one birder who carries a pocket recorder for this and for taping hotlines over the phone, eliminating the need to call back if he misses crucial information.

The spotted owl, the western counterpart of the barred owl, presents special owl-finding problems. Because it is a federally listed endan-

In the old-growth forest of the Pacific Northwest, *top*, the location of spotted owls is best kept secret, in order to avoid undue disturbance.

gered species, under no conditions should one be harassed. Never use tapes for spotted owl finding. Not only might it disturb the birds, but it is also illegal unless special permits have been acquired for official surveys.

Spotted owls can, however, be seen. There is a well-known pair that has been viewed by hundreds, if not thousands of avid birders, in Garden Canyon in the Huachuca Mountains in Arizona. In Arizona, they are found in mixed oak-coniferous forests in narrow canyons with nearby streams. Again, no tapes, but ask other birders if and where the owls have been seen. Do not attempt to get close for photographs. Content yourself with a good look from a distance.

Some pairs of spotted owls in southern and central California are reportedly fairly easy to see. They live in dense woodlands in steep-sided canyons and shady ravines, usually near a stream. Consult regional bird-finding guides.

In the Pacific Northwest, the spotted owl's old-growth stronghold, do not expect them to be on hotlines. Here, their locations are a closely guarded conservation secret, since some have been shot by loggers. Because of the huge controversy over the logging of the old-growth temperate rain forest in the Pacific Northwest, any spotted owl you find should remain confidential and be reported only to reputable conservation groups or U.S. Fish and Wildlife Service officials.

An ultimate quest of birders, the great gray owl rarely leaves its far-northern haunts.

Great Gray Owl

Strix nebulosa
Length: 28"
Wingspan: 54"

Few birds create as much excitement among birders as the great gray owl. It does not matter how many great grays one has seen (and few have seen many), the report of one within driving distance almost always causes any birder who has ever chased this owl to cancel appointments and rearrange schedules. A great gray owl is one of the ultimate quests.

We saw our first great grays (five in all) during the Amherst Island invasion in the winter of 1983-84. We took off from work, packed the car and pushed off from New Jersey early one Sunday morning. We arrived in southeastern Ontario eight hours later with about an hour of daylight left. Forgetting about the motel reservations, we immediately followed directions friends had given us. We ventured into the snowy farm fields outside Kingston and soon came upon a jumble of cars and a knot of birders, all shuffling their feet. We knew we were in the right spot, but no one was looking through binoculars or telescopes. "You should have been here this morning" was the dreary consensus. "The birds haven't been seen since 8:00 a.m." We decided to drive around, get the lay of the land and see what kind of country these great grays had chosen.

We had driven down the road exactly one mile, when Pat said, "I might have one. There's a silhouette on the top of a snag against the far tree line." A quick check revealed a great gray. We returned to the spot where the cluster of birders had been, but they had left, so we went back, set up scopes and enjoyed the bird, occasionally scanning for others. A second great gray, dangling a large rodent, flew in and perched in the same tree line. We watched them until darkness fell an hour later.

As the full moon rose on that first day, we were treated to an entirely unexpected bonus. Deep, low "whooo whooo whooo" calls drifted across the fields; it was a great gray calling. Great horned owls began calling simultaneously, one from an exposed perch on top of a giant snag.

Thus began a four-day vacation among the owls that had invaded the Kingston/Amherst Island area. Over the course of that winter, the area attracted seven great grays, over fifteen snowys, one barred, over fifteen long-eareds, ten saw-whets and two boreal owls.

Forced out of the frozen, foodless north, these birds had been attracted to and concentrated by a meadow vole population explosion on Amherst Island. As we walked across a pasture, voles scattered with every step. Hungry owls (in many cases starving), pushed out of their normal winter range by a lack of food, had migrated along the north shore of Lake Ontario and found this plethora of rodents. The numbers of hawks and owls grew throughout the season, peaking in late February.

Only during such an irruption are you likely to see a great gray south of its normal range. Usually nonmigratory, great gray owls breed in boreal forests and wooded bogs of the far

Great gray owls raise their young in the boreal forests and wooded bogs of the far north.

88

Usually nonmigratory, great grays are occasionally driven south by food shortages.

north, from Ontario west to British Columbia and Alaska.

During many winter seasons, no great grays are reported south of their range. Some winters, just one or two reports are received. Major irruptions have occurred just three times in the past 20 years. The 1978-79 flight was concentrated largely in southern Ontario, southern Quebec, New York and Maine, with over 334 birds recorded. The 1983-84 irruption was even larger, with nearly 1,000 birds reported, most of them in Ontario and Quebec, as well as significant numbers in Manitoba and New York. The 1991-92 owl flight was largely confined to the western Great Lakes. (Minnesota also had a major flight during the winter of 1990-91.) In Sault Ste. Marie, Michigan, at least 59 great gray owls, 23 hawk owls and many snowy owls were drawn to the area. The following winter, 16 great gray owls returned to this area.

When will it happen again? Dictated by food shortages in the north and ample food concentrations in the south, no one really knows when the next flight may be. They generally do not begin until December or January, and peak in late February and early March (with sightings lasting until mid-April). The 1991-92 Michigan irruption, however, dwindled by February, due to disappearing food concentrations and possi-

Although they can be spotted at twilight, great grays usually prefer to hunt by night.

bly pressure from birders, photographers and researchers.

If you wish to see a great gray owl, be ready for an invasion year. Plan to drop everything for a northern midwinter vacation. When flights occur, or even a single great gray appears, hotlines will have the latest information and birders' phones will be ringing with reports. Follow hotline directions and ask local birders for up-to-date information.

Plan to be out at dawn and dusk, when your chances of finding them hunting are best. While great gray owls hunt mainly at night, they may also hunt at dawn until about 10:00 a.m., and again at dusk—coming out at about 4:00 p.m.

If hungry and hunting, they may sit out in the open throughout an overcast day. Though they can be difficult to spot at midday even when present, scan all potential perches for their large shape. (They are huge—North America's largest owl in overall size.) They may be on the top of a tree, but are more often perched lower in the branches. Some may perch deep in evergreens and be remarkably camouflaged for such a large owl. Look especially along roadsides, in clearings and at the edges of fields. In flight, great grays move very low over the landscape, like other owls, then swoop way up to a prominent perch. Their wings are immense—very long with wide feathers.

If you do not wish to wait for an irruption to view this great bird, there are several places where the great gray owl's breeding range is accessible to the average birder or traveler. For several years, pairs have nested in northern Minnesota, some near Duluth, and have been found there with some regularity by tour guides and birding tour groups. Consult birding tour companies and check birding guide classified advertisements in birding magazines to learn of organized trips in this region. *A Birder's Guide to Minnesota*, by Kim Eckert, thoroughly covers this region if you want to bird it on your own.

Great gray owls also nest, uncommonly, in dense coniferous forests and meadows of the western mountains—in the Rocky Mountains of Montana and Wyoming and in the Pacific Cascade Range in Washington and Oregon. Birds here are few and largely inaccessible. Ask local birders about great gray owls if you are traveling to these areas.

Great gray owls nest regularly at Yosemite National Park, in the Sierra Nevada Mountains of central California. Here a few pairs nest securely. Birding tour groups see them regularly, as do some guided park nature tours. To see a great gray here, consider going with an organized birding tour group or ask park naturalists where to look for the

Some great grays nest in northern Minnesota and in mountainous regions in some parts of the West.

birds. Because it is a national park, luring owls with tapes is not permitted. This is the case in all national parks and many state parks. Besides, tapes are reported to have little or no effect in attracting great grays.

Eastern Screech Owl

Otus asio
Length: 8"
Wingspan: 21"

Perhaps you have heard the eerie whinny or wail of a screech owl, a surprise to those who expect their call to sound more like their name. In fact, it is the barn owl whose call is more of a screech.

The screech owl is one of our smallest birds of prey and has two color forms, gray and red, although in the East a distinctly brown intergrade seems to occur. Some books refer to these as phases or morphs. A single brood of young may contain several of each color. The color difference does not change throughout a bird's life and is often said to have nothing to do with the bird's sex, although an 1890s study in the Philadelphia area showed that 92 percent of red birds were female and 89 percent of gray birds were male.

Screech owls are common breeding birds throughout the East and are found in rural areas, woodlots, small towns and even city parks. Like great horned and barred owls, these nonmigratory birds are far less common at the northern edge of their range.

These owls nest in tree cavities, deserted woodpecker holes and even man-made boxes, including wood-duck boxes. They particularly favor old apple orchards, since the knurled apple trees sport many holes. (Too few landowners realize the value of standing dead trees to hole-nesting birds. Where dead trees have been left standing, there is commonly a gathering of summer tanagers, red-headed woodpeckers, blue-birds and screech owls. About 85 species of birds and 45 species of mammals commonly use tree cavities in the United States.)

Check every hole in a tree, particularly those facing the sun, during cold weather. It may take a while, but eventually you will be rewarded by a camouflaged shape sitting at the entrance to its home. Once we even spotted an eastern screech owl while traveling 50 miles per hour on a major road. A red blob in a hole in a tree became, after a U-turn and binocular check, a red screech owl catching some rays.

Once discovered, you will find certain holes produce again and again. In New Jersey, at Rancocas Nature Center, a screech owl sat in the sun almost every winter day for over two years, and was enjoyed by hundreds of people. Pete Dunne saw a screech owl in the same red cedar near his house every few days over the course of an entire winter, after initially finding it by following up mobbing songbirds.

A lesser known fact about screech owls is that they often roost in evergreens—dense pines or, particularly, red cedars. On a few occasions, we have been alerted to

One of the smallest birds of prey, the screech owl nests in tree cavities and has two color forms, gray and red.

As young screech owls outgrow the nest, they may be found huddled together on a branch.

their presence by mobbing chickadees and titmice. Be alert for the strident calling of agitated songbirds. Then proceed very slowly to the spot, scanning every likely tree (or hole) as you go. Some evergreen roost sites, like certain holes, are favored over time.

Because they are exclusively nocturnal, screech owls are virtually never seen except in the circumstances just described. Luckily, however, screech owls are easily lured in. Of all the owls, screech owls seem to respond best to taping. Many people find a whistled imitation of their call works just as well, which is much more convenient in the field. Listen to records or tapes, then practice the "whinny" at home. It may take a while to perfect your call, but try it next time in the field and you may find yourself talking to a screech owl.

Usually it only takes a few minutes for a screech owl to respond if it is in the area. They may even respond during the daytime, though usually this will happen only on a dark or overcast day. At night, they often fly in to investigate. For best results, get down on your knees or with your back to vegetation (to break up your obvious silhouette). Acclimate your eyes to the dark, then begin calling. Once you hear a response, watch for movement or a silhouette against the sky. Then find the owl in your flashlight beam. Often a screech owl will sit quietly, almost demurely, in the beam of a light, seemingly oblivious to how visible it is. Usually a screech owl will call first, but sometimes they fly in undetected, so be alert for any situation.

It seems somewhat unusual that screech owls respond so well to active luring, since they are not a particularly vocal owl. We have two pairs by our home, one in the backyard and one down the street, yet we only hear them less than once a month.

Western Screech Owl

Otus kennicottii
Length: 8"
Wingspan: 21"

A close relative and counterpart of the eastern screech owl, the western screech owl is largely indistinguishable from it in the field, though no true red forms of the western species occur (some in the coastal northwest are quite brownish). There are very few areas in which the two species overlap, but if they do, their specific calls are the best clue to separating them. The western screech owl has a "bouncing ball" call—short whistles accelerating in tempo. Some have said that the western screech owl does not respond as well to imitations, but perhaps this is because the whistle is harder to duplicate.

Once, on a bitter cold but quiet winter night in the Chiricahua Mountains of southern Arizona, we worked the hillside juniper patches with bird artist and tour guide Dave Sibley, looking for western screech owls. After hearing them from camp while cooking dinner, we tracked them down to a specific patch of scrub.

They responded immediately to Dave's whistling. Two birds came quite close but were maddeningly hard to see, staying just out of sight in the dense foliage, unlike many confiding eastern screech owls we have seen.

Whiskered Screech Owl

Otus trichopsis
Length: 7"
Wingspan: 18"

The whiskered screech owl closely resembles the gray form of the western screech owl. Here, too, identification must be made by voice. While the western screech owl is found at lower elevations (in open woodlands, streamside forests, parks and arid areas), the whiskered screech owl is a high-altitude dweller, only found in dense oak and oak-conifer woodlands above 4,000 feet in elevation. In these rich forests, their staccato Morse code-like duets may be heard.

Common in Mexico, the whiskered screech owl reaches the northern limit of its range in southeast Arizona. Again, memorize the calls from tapes or records to prepare yourself for hearing them when you visit their specific native habitats in their limited range in the southwest.

Flammulated Owl

Otus flammeolus
Length: 6"
Wingspan: 16"

Another member of the *Otus* or screech owl group, the flammulated owl is considerably smaller than other screech owls: 6 inches in length compared to 8 inches for the western screech owl. This species also has both a red and a gray form; the more northerly birds are generally grayer.

Unlike other screech owls, the flammulated owl is highly migratory. It breeds from Washington and Oregon south through Mexico, but completely withdraws from its North American breeding range in winter. Because of its long-distance migrations, it has been recorded as a rare vagrant in Florida, Louisiana and eastern Texas.

The flammulated owl is common in parts of its range. It occurs in mountain forests within stands of ponderosa and Jeffrey pines. Like other screech owls, it is nocturnal, roosting either in cavities or dense foliage, and it is best located by its call. Flammulateds will respond to either tape recordings or an imitation of their single or

Left: **Western screech owls inhabit lower elevations in open woodlands and arid areas.**

Above: **Unlike others in the screech owl family, the flammulated owl is highly migratory.**

paired hoots. Remember they are migratory, so early spring or early fall is the obvious time to try actively luring them with tapes—not summer, when they are breeding.

Northern Saw-Whet Owl

Aegolius acadicus
Length: 8"
Wingspan: 19"

The saw-whet owl, named for one of its calls—a repeated metallic note that was originally likened to the whetting (or sharpening) of a saw—is largely a northerner, breeding from the Appalachian Mountains of West Virginia and Pennsylvania, north to Nova Scotia in the East and west through the northern Great Lakes states and central Canada to the Alaskan Coast. It is migratory, heading south in fall to escape the deep winter snows. While a few spend the winter north through Maine and Minnesota, perhaps never leaving their breeding territories, many head south for warmer climates. They prey on small rodents, such as voles, shrews and woodland species of mice, as well as frogs and insects when available.

One day in late October, Pat arrived at the Cape May Point State Park at first light. The night before had been quite cold and crystal clear. Each star shimmered and just a sliver of the moon illuminated the sky. A strong cold front had passed several days

---

Largely northern breeders, the tiny saw-whets migrate south in the fall.

before and finally the winds, although still from the north, had dropped to a gentle breeze. The conditions were perfect for migrating owls.

Pat could hear her heart pounding as she walked the wooden boardwalk through the bayberry, cedar, holly and honeysuckle tangles. She rounded a bend in the trail and a silent, dark shape flushed. Continuing more slowly and cautiously now, she rounded another bend. Ahead, a long-eared returned her surprised look from its perch in a tangle overhanging the trail. Its attention seemed to be focused more off to the side than on her. When she turned to look into the catbrier thicket  next to her, a wide-eyed saw-whet blinked back. Each owl flew silently off after a fraction of a moment. Before the morning hawk flight was underway, Pat had seen ten or more owls as she crept silently through the trails.

Each fall, from late September through mid-November, hundreds, if not thousands, of saw-whet owls migrate south, concentrating at migrant traps like Duluth, Minnesota, Whitefish Point, Michigan, and Cape May, New Jersey. Each spring, from mid-March to early May, hundreds migrate north, concentrating in places like Braddock Bay, New York, and Whitefish Point, Michigan. Full-time owl banding projects at each of these locations have

In breeding season, owlers should be content to listen to the calls of saw-whet owls.

found saw-whets to be the most common owl migrant.

The key to finding migrant owls is to play the weather and put energy and time into looking for them after a good migration night. Katy Duffy of the Cape May Owl Banding Project has found that, in the fall, good nights for owl migration are clear, still nights with gentle north or northwest winds that follow a cold front. Similar conditions stimulate owl flights through Duluth, where up to 292 owls have been recorded in a single night by researchers at Hawk Ridge Nature Reserve. Jeff Dodge, who works at Braddock Bay Raptor Research, has found that good owl migration in spring is triggered by light southerly winds and a warming trend, with a low-pressure system approaching.

Saw-whets can end up anywhere during migration. Some have landed on ships, others have shown up in yards to roost in an evergreen near an active bird feeder; even luckier ones find preserves where there is plenty of habitat and food.

At Cape May, we have learned to be the first ones to walk the nature trails after a good migration night. Our reward after many, many tries has been close encounters with owls like the morning described above. We have frequently found owls perched in overhangs or dense evergreens right next to the trail. Apparently, they are attracted to perches next to the open areas created by the pathways in an otherwise dense habitat. The first person through the trails, though, alerts the owls to their vulnerability and they instantly flush deeper in, not to be seen again.

A few times we've had the opportunity to watch a saw-whet fly: it flew dead away on very rapid wing beats, reminding us of a woodcock. While hunting, they no doubt do quite a bit of gliding like other owls.

At Duluth, migrant saw-whets occasionally roost in the pines in and around Hawk Ridge Nature Reserve from late September to mid-October. At Braddock Bay, they roost in the few stands of evergreens. So that you do not disrupt these roosts, take advantage of organized owl walks offered from mid-March through April.

Finding saw-whet owls on the breeding grounds and finding them in their winter quarters takes two completely different approaches. Spotting saw-whets in winter, when they spread over much of the United States from South Carolina west to Texas, involves a great deal of physical searching. Evergreens, such as pines, firs, junipers, cedars, hollies and rhododendrons, offer the best cover. Groves of evergreens or small, dense stands are best, particularly when surrounded by deciduous woodlots or, better yet, open country.

We once found a saw-whet in a red cedar in a cemetery in Kansas. The nearest woods were over seven miles away along a stream. Pine or cedar groves in coastal dune areas also harbor wintering saw-whets. Check for telltale pellets and whitewash under any dense grove of younger-growth conifers. The height at which the birds perch can vary greatly, from 20 to 30 feet to (more often) at or below eye-level—wherever the densest vegetation offers the best concealment from daytime predators.

In some parts of the country the search is complicated, if not made impossible, by extensive stands of evergreens. At one roost on the Delaware River, saw-whets perch in Virginia pines, red cedars, a dense stand of young white pines, honeysuckle vines, catbrier tangles and even oak trees where clumps of dead leaves still linger on the tree. The same roost sites, even specific branches, are used again and again, sometimes year after year.

On National Audubon Society Christmas Bird Counts, we always spend an hour or two trying for saw-whet owls. Try it

Finding saw-whets in the winter requires searching through evergreens and other dense cover.

yourself—play their song for three to five minutes, then listen for five minutes, then play again, then listen again. Some birders memorize the call and can whistle it perfectly. While sometimes you will be rewarded with the classic "toot-toot-toot" call, be forewarned that saw-whets have a variety of calls not recorded on retail records and tapes. One response is a wail described by some as screech-owl like, others sound vaguely like a barred owl. A common response that we call the "challenge call" is a catlike whine or yelp, which rises in tone at the end. It is fairly soft, like a catbird's call or that of a yellow-bellied sapsucker.

If you hear this (or other calls) close by, sweep the area with your flashlight to find the challenger. Also, do not automatically assume a respondent is of the same species; we have had saw-whets respond to screech owl tapes, and particularly screech owls to saw-whet tapes. Territories of various owl species can overlap, and a bird may respond to a potential competitor.

Unless you are part of a bona fide survey effort, do not play tapes during the breeding season. On the breeding grounds, passive listening is the best way to find owls. At Whitefish Point, Michigan, breeding saw-whets arrive in late March. Males begin calling then to advertise the nest site they have chosen. By early May the calling stops, perhaps coinciding with the arrival of females to the breeding sites. In breeding areas, be content with hearing them; do not feel you have to see them. Choose a quiet, windless night to listen, and choose the habitat carefully.

Topographic maps are the best way to find potential owl habitats. For saw-whets, look for coniferous forests, mixed forests, wooded swamps and bogs. Beaver ponds and flows are often good areas to try because a good mix of habitats is created and standing dead (hollow) trees are prime nest sites. In parts of Wyoming, look in aspen groves because this is where flickers nest and saw-whets often use old flicker cavities.

Boreal Owl

Aegolius funereus
Length: 10"
Wingspan: 22"

Except for those in Alaska and the small populations breeding in Minnesota and high in the Rocky Mountains, the boreal owl is a Canadian citizen. It is generally nonmigratory and breeds in muskeg bogs and dense northern forests from Labrador west to the Northwest Territories, the Yukon and Alaska. Much of its range is largely inaccessible to birders. Luckily, though, the boreal owl is irruptive. Almost every year, a few wander south of the breeding range, no doubt in response to localized absence of prey.

To see a boreal owl you must usually follow hotline reports of irruptions. Recently, one spent an entire winter in a cedar grove in Connecticut and was seen by many hun-

Largely confined to Canada and Alaska, boreal owls may come south only during irruptions.

dreds of birders. The 1983-84 Amherst Island owl invasion in southeastern Ontario included several boreal owls, although when we visited, the abundance of birders had caused them to move. Each spring for the past few years, banders at Braddock Bay Raptor Research have seen or heard several boreal owls. These birds, along the Lake Ontario shore, are proof that at least a few make it south into New York State almost every winter.

Whitefish Point, Michigan, is perhaps the best place to spot boreal owls. The Whitefish Point Bird Observatory has banded over 400 since 1983, with a high of 163 banded in the spring of 1988. Boreal owls migrate north through Whitefish Point in April and early May, with peak numbers occurring there about every four years. Observatory researchers suggest looking for them in late April and early May (when numbers are greatest) roosting in jack pines just south of the Point. Ask observatory staff for up-to-date information.

Be alert for saw-whet and long-eared owls while prowling for roosting boreals, since good numbers of each also migrate through each spring. In fall, you will find saw-whets in these same areas.

With all this in mind, birders in wild

places like Maine, northern Vermont, New York, Minnesota and particularly Michigan have nothing to lose by trying for boreal owls a few times each winter and spring. It takes an act of faith, but try tapping on trees with holes for possible boreal owls on Christmas Bird Counts and other winter excursions. Use tape calls for them much as you would for a saw-whet or screech owl. Listen for their rich whistled notes rising at the end, like a winnowing snipe. They are probably more likely to answer in early spring, just before they leave for their breeding grounds.

Do not use tapes in known Rocky Mountain breeding areas. Here, boreals may be quite rare, perhaps with only a tenuous breeding foothold, and should not be continually disrupted by birders. If you live within their breeding range, consider putting up nest boxes to attract them. Use the standard box for American kestrels and screech owls, but make the entrance hole larger: 3½ inches.

Boreal owls are strictly nocturnal. They roost during daylight hours in dense cover, usually conifers, or in holes in trees. Search for them in daytime as you would for saw-whet or long-eared owls. The boreal owl is larger than a saw-whet (10 inches versus 8 inches), but for positive identification you must see the chocolate brown streaking (the saw-whet is reddish brown), the darker back (compared to the saw-whet), the black markings on the edge of the facial disk and particularly the yellow or pale-colored bill.

Perhaps your best chance to see a boreal owl is to go on an Alaskan or northern Minnesota trip in summer. Only here are breeding populations large enough and accessible enough that you have a reasonably good chance of finding them. In Minnesota, breeding males begin to call in February to attract a mate to their chosen nest site, but get quiet as soon as females arrive. During the vocal period, males sing nonstop through the night from their nest cavity. The song may sound soft and faraway, since they sing from inside the cavity.

Hawk Ridge Nature Reserve in Duluth, Minnesota, offers a "Boreal Owl Birding Weekend" each year in either late March or early April to Superior National Forest, northeast of Duluth, where boreal owls breed. Weather permitting, boreal owls can be easily heard and, with luck, sometimes seen (saw-whets are also likely,

Usually nonmigratory, boreal owls breed in muskeg bogs and dense northern forests.

and sometimes even great grays, northern hawk owls and long-eared owls). In recent years, a number of birding tour companies have "staked out" boreal owls as part of their Alaskan itineraries. While nothing is guaranteed, this is a very good way to increase your chances of adding boreal owls to your life list. Call the tour companies and ask if boreal (along with great grays and hawk owls) can be expected as part of the itinerary.

Boreal owls are not particularly rare, but, as their name implies, they are probably less accessible than any other North American owl species. Adding a sighting to your life list will be a special memory when you are successful.

With its crepuscular habits and a preference for open habitat, the short-eared owl is one of the easiest to spot.

Short-Eared Owl

Asio flammeus
Length: 15"
Wingspan: 41"

Short-eared owls were at one time common breeding birds on the coastal salt marshes in the East. In New Jersey in recent years, not a single nest has been found. Man-made changes to marshes (filling, draining and alteration) have certainly had an impact on their presence. By mid-October there is an influx as those from breeding populations in the north migrate south. They move in and populate the tidal salt marshes, often perching on hay bales, fence posts or the marsh itself.

Of all the owls except the burrowing owl, the short-eared owl is the easiest to watch during the day. While a fairly uncommon breeder in the lower 48 states, short-eareds can be numerous as a wintering bird, in proper habitat, throughout most of the country.

To find short-eared owls, first find their preferred open country haunts: tundra, marshes, large weedy fields, meadows and prairies. During bright, sunny days and particularly when it is cold and windy, they

Though breeding numbers have dropped, the short-eared can be a fairly common winter bird.

time. We suspect the preceding day's weather, prey availability and even tides in coastal areas play a factor as to when they hunt.

Look for the short-eared owl's low, coursing flight. If you find hunting northern harriers ("marsh hawks"), you are in the right place. Harriers and short-eareds usually share the same hunting and nesting grounds. Harriers will fly with their wings slightly raised over the back, in a dihedral. Short-eareds hold their wings flat, or slightly drooped, when hunting. Look for the barrellike, headless shape to separate short-eareds from distant harriers. The short-eared owl's flight is buoyant—they are reminiscent of a giant moth in flight.

Don't always expect short-eared owls to fly low over the landscape. Sometimes they fly quite high, and sometimes they hover while hunting. Perhaps once or twice a winter we see short-eareds actually soaring high up, circling with harriers and rough-legged hawks. On some occasions, it may be quiet enough to hear the short-eared owl's call—a high pitched bark not unlike the yap of a small dog. They call repeatedly during the nesting season. In winter, hunting short-eareds will sometimes call when they encounter one another or when they interact with hunting northern harriers.

Short-eareds on occasion migrate during the day, and are sometimes spotted at coastal hawk migration watches—one or

perch inconspicuously out of the elements. In late afternoon, however, they become very active, and perch low but conspicuously on signs, stakes, hay mounds, muskrat houses and duck blinds. On quiet, cloudy, often warmer days, they are sometimes seen flying at midday. In fact, except during high winds, you may find a short-eared at any two each fall at Cape May, New Jersey, and one or two each spring at Sandy Hook, New Jersey. A few are seen regularly each spring at the Braddock Bay Hawk Watch near Rochester, New York.

Where short-eareds nest, look for the male doing his courtship display, where he shows off the undersides of his wings, which are very white with dark wingtips. This often occurs before sunset.

On more than one occasion, we have found roosting short-eareds by simply walking back and forth across the open marshes. On one memorable Christmas Bird Count, a lengthy hike across frozen marshes flushed ten short-eared owls, all from within a one-acre roosting area. Once a roost is located, you can watch it from a safe, nonintrusive distance on subsequent afternoons.

Another method is to try squeaking. If a short-eared is hunting nearby, try imitating an injured rodent. Many will respond instantly, coming close to investigate. Using a car as a blind works best for this, and we have had them hover outside the window, wondering where the mouse was! If you are taking pictures, be ready. They will only be fooled once, and their investigation will last only a few moments.

The short-eared owl is one of the easier owls to study because it is one of the most active during daylight hours and, for most of North America, it is one of the most accessible owls. From the winter marshes of Newburyport, Massachusetts, down through New Jersey's Atlantic coast and Delaware Bay marshes, and from the prairies of Squaw Creek National Wildlife Refuge in Missouri and Buffalo Lake in Texas, to the Sulphur Springs Valley in Arizona, short-eared owls can provide the watcher with hours of study. With many owls, even a good look may last only a few minutes. Short-eareds, however, can provide insight into an owl's world as you get to watch them hunt, catch mice, interact with one another, chase off harriers, perch and preen. For these reasons, this is a good owl to focus on when you begin your owl-watching career.

Long-Eared Owl

Asio otus
Length: 14"
Wingspan: 39"

If the short-eared owl is the easiest to spot, the long-eared owl is one of the hardest. A forest dweller to begin with, the long-eared is also shy, reticent, secretive and easily flushed. It is strictly nocturnal and quite uncommon over much of its breeding range. It is widespread, however, nesting from the Gaspé Peninsula west to Alberta in Canada, and south through Oklahoma to California.

The highly secretive long-eared owl is rarely seen except in winter when it is gregarious and roosts communally in dense groves of evergreen trees. Often perched

against a tree trunk, a long-eared's streaked form becomes one with the bark. This streaked chest and the ability (like other owls) to go from a plump shape to a very elongated shape when alarmed helps camouflage long-eared owls. Even the ear tufts topping this shape add to the overall illusion of looking like a tree stump rather than an owl.

Hunting through dark forests for such a camouflaged creature is made easier by the presence of their gleaming white excrement. Like saw-whets, long-eareds will return from their nightly forays to the very same daytime roost tree, even the same spot on the same branch. Often the ground beneath an owl roost is littered with pellets. The same spot may be used all winter, year after year.

Searching for long-eared owls involves penetrating the densest tangles and the thickest groves of junipers and cedars. In the East, this can be difficult, due to the abundance and continuity of the forests. In the tree-poor plains and desert states, however, this search is much easier. Check any available stands of planted pines, junipers or other evergreens.

Since they are easily flushed, you must go through a grove very slowly and quietly, carefully scanning each tree ahead, looking for the elongated, camouflaged shape of this owl. Stop frequently to look ahead with your naked eye and to scan with binoculars. Look for its form perched close to a tree trunk

or for fresh whitewash dripping down through dense evergreens. If you are lucky, you can follow the trail of whitewash up the tree to a solid owl form.

We have heard tales of long-eared owls growing accustomed to people and becoming "tame" after repeated visits. In our experience, long-eareds only get more wary upon each encounter with man. And since gun-toting hunters share the woods with binocular-toting birders, this is a good thing. A long-eared owl that had been banded at Cape May during the fall migration was shot by a hunter in New Brunswick, Canada, several years later. The last thing any of us should want is for an owl to grow accustomed to man.

Once in a while, reasonably "tame" (we prefer "unthreatened") long-eared owls are

A shy forest dweller, the long-eared owl, *left*, is difficult to spot. For raising their broods, they favor abandoned raptor or squirrel nests, *above*.

Until young owls can fly, they walk around on branches near the nest, often huddled together.

slowly, but never closer.

We find that in dense tangles, the moment of discovery, of first visibility through the shrubs, is probably the minimum safe distance. Then quietly watch the bird—speak only in whispers. Ideally, the bird will then relax, becoming less wary. We have seen them slowly relax their elongated camouflage posture and assume a puffed-out sleepy posture. On one memorable occasion, a long-eared owl even regurgitated a pellet while we watched.

Long-eared owls can seldom be spotted on their breeding grounds. They are uncommon, even rare, throughout their breeding range, and they are not very vocal compared to other owls. Listen to records and familiarize yourself with the male's "hoo" call given at dusk. They use abandoned raptor or squirrel nests, which are usually compact and in deciduous trees and are usually smaller than those used by great horned owls. Finding a long-eared owl nest in the northeastern states is one of the most thrilling finds a naturalist can make.

found. Then, with care, people can view the birds repeatedly, sometimes over the course of several months.

Long-eared owls are decidedly colonial in winter roosts. When you find one, there are probably more, either in the same or adjacent trees. If you spot a long-eared owl that has not flushed, do not move closer. Do everything in slow motion. If branches are in the way of a clear view, move laterally,

Because of their rarity and retiring nature, you should never use tapes to find long-eareds unless you are involved in an official survey, breeding bird census or Christmas Bird Count.

Long-eared owls are the second most common owl migrant, following saw-whets, at migrant traps like Cape May, New Jersey, and Duluth, Minnesota, in the fall, and at Braddock Bay, New York, and Whitefish Point, Michigan, in the spring. Because of their exclusively nocturnal habits, they are virtually never seen at dawn or dusk except during migration. But at both Cape May and Whitefish Point, observers scanning the treetops from elevated vantage points have, on occasion, watched long-eareds and other owls leave their daytime roosts to begin their nocturnal migration. The magic time is dusk until full darkness. Look for them as they lift off from the woods against the last light of sunset, circling higher and higher and moving farther and farther out.

During migration, observers have had some luck "squeaking" for long-eareds. Once attracted by imitated cries of injured prey, birds were then watched as they hunted while bathed in the light of a full moon.

Barn Owl

Tyto alba
Length: 17"
Wingspan: 44"

The dark grove of cedars on the edge of the Delaware Bay marshes near Goshen, New Jersey, seemed lifeless. We thought it would be just one more winter walk through a still and quiet landscape, until we came upon a scattered pile of owl pellets and whitewash. Overhead, an out-of-place solid form became apparent in the latticework of dark evergreen branches. The heart-shaped face, pale cinnamon underparts with black-pepper spots and butterscotch-colored back with darker delicate tones told us it was a barn owl. We sank down to the ground and slowly eased our binoculars up for a lengthy, priceless look. The owl's eyes appeared closed, squeezed shut, but as we inched sideways for a better view, its head turned ever so slowly to face us.

The barn owl is strictly nocturnal and seldom seen except when found at its daytime roost. Over the years we have seen a few, but only their ghostly pale mothlike shapes crossing through the beam of the Cape May Point Lighthouse during the fall migration. Since barn owls are the most vocal of all that migrate through Cape May each fall, our clue then was their bone-chilling shriek of a call.

Our clue that day beside Delaware Bay was the telltale pellets—about 15 of them—indicating that the owl had been there just over two weeks. If we were lucky, it would remain throughout the entire winter, feeding on the bay marshes' abundant meadow vole population.

Not wanting the moment to end, but realizing that a full minute of observation may have already disturbed the bird, we slowly inched away. The very small, diminutive shape slowly fluffed out and elongated; the black eyes opened wide. Its predator alertness erased the soft mood of the dark woods. It dropped from the branch and flew away through a maze of dense cedar trees. Not a sound was made.

Hunters, trappers and landowners wander though similar cedar groves and pine woods, but few ever see the groups of barn and long-eared owls that may roost in them—sometimes a dozen or more. Winter is one of the few seasons when these secretive creatures may be found and studied because of their tendency at that time to roost communally in groups.

The most intensive barn owl population study in the world is currently under way in southwestern New Jersey. The study of nesting birds was initiated in 1980, and since then nearly 2,000 young from this study area have been banded. Bruce Colvin and Paul Hegdal, principal researchers in this study, report that today the majority of nest sites are in the barn owl boxes they placed in barns, silos and other man-made structures.

In 1985, the study found seven nests in large hollow trees along the main street of Greenwich, in Cumberland County, New Jersey. During the peak of the nesting season, when the young are always hungry and, come nightfall, quite vocal with their raspy, food-begging demands, the residents of this town are very aware of their presence. Otherwise, though, you might not even know they are there, sequestered in the huge sycamores and silver maples that line the main street. This impressive population seems to be due to the rich expanses of the Delaware Bay and River marshes (which teem with meadow voles, a favored food of the barn owl) coupled with southwest New Jersey's dairy farm areas and associated grassland habitat, where barn owls can forage.

The barn owl is cosmopolitan in its choice of habitat, and in North

Although widely distributed, the barn owl is nocturnal and seldom seen except when found at its daytime roost.

The raspy begging of barn owl chicks can be easily heard, especially on a still night.

America it is widely, if spottily, distributed. Northern populations, such as those in New York State and southern Wisconsin, appear migratory—New York birds have been found as far south as Florida. Each fall, migrant barn owls are banded at Cape May. In the 1970s and early 1980s, they were Cape May's second most common migrant owl. In recent years, very few have been banded, but many still pass over—their screeching call readily gives away their presence.

To find barn owls, start by looking in areas with the grassland or marsh habitats that these birds require. Once the habitat is located, then focus on possible nest and roost sites—listen at night and talk with locals. Colvin and Hegdal found that barn owls range one to two miles between their nest site and good feeding habitat.

To spot barn owls, you must use a number of different methods, so varied is their choice of roost and nest sites. In farm country, where there are grasslands and nearby marshes, ask friendly farmers if barn owls are present; they may know of just the barn, silo, chimney or tree where you may get a look at one. Often abandoned buildings, even urban structures like warehouses, hold barn owls, but for safety's sake we do not recommend venturing into these. Church steeples have a long and colorful history of

Barn owls often nest in abandoned buildings, even warehouses, if they can find a way in.

being readily used by barn owls.

Once owls are found, they can be watched coming and going night after night. One abandoned schoolhouse held a pair of barn owls for years, and we could watch them enter and leave the cupola by the light of nearby street lamps. Keep in mind, however, that the most common nest and roost sites in the East are in trees.

In western states, caves and holes in cliffs are commonly used by barn owls. In Mexico, we saw them in large caves that we visited while conducting bat research. On a trip to Arizona's Sulphur Springs Valley with bird artist Dave Sibley, we were stumped as to where we might find barn owls. The Christmas Bird Count listed them as numerous, yet there were few conifers, no cliffs and few abandoned farm buildings.

Local bird expert Arnie Moorhouse grinned when we asked about barn owls and guided us to them. We stopped at the end of a dirt road and began walking across an open farm field with no structure or vegetation higher than two feet in sight. "Right over here," Arnie said, and before we even saw the depression in the ground, a barn owl flushed in front of us. Here, in the Arizona grasslands, barn owls commonly roost in abandoned mine shafts—below ground.

Katy Duffy, director of Cape May's Owl Banding Project, has observed quite a few barn owls hunting and migrating during her dusk-to-dawn net checks. Barn owls in flight remind her of flying manta rays due to their short tails.

Because they are exclusively nocturnal, barn owls are seldom seen at dawn or dusk except during migration, yet on two occasions we were treated to a lengthy look at barn owls hunting in broad daylight. Once, in January, we watched a barn owl hunt for about an hour at 10:00 a.m. over the prairie at Cape Sable in the Everglades National Park in Florida. Another time, in December, a barn owl was hunting over the New Jersey salt marshes at 3:00 p.m., coursing the meadows much like a short-eared owl. Birds exhibiting this behavior are either stressed or have hungry young mouths to feed, a possibility even in winter as barn owls may nest any month of the year.

Very few people in North America are familiar with barn owl sounds and that, combined with their nocturnal behavior, is a prime reason why they frequently go undetected. Passive listening is a good way to find barn owls. The loud, raspy begging of chicks, particularly near fledging time, can easily be heard on a still night. Adult barn owls give a short screech or eeeklike sound as they traverse their range. Barn owls also can give a blood-curdling scream when their nests are approached. They make such a wide variety of noises, from squeaking to screaming, that unidentifiable sounds at night in barn owl country may well be some of their vast repertoire of calls.

Most methods for spotting other owls work for barn owls as well. In winter, barn owls commonly roost in dense evergreens, so search for them using the same methods we have suggested for long-eareds and saw-whets. Also, barn owls will nest and roost in large, hollow trees. Check these as well, searching for telltale signs—a downy feather at the hole's entrance or pellets on the ground. Finally, "squeaking" seems to work well for barn owls (although using tapes does not). Employ this as you might for short-eared or long-eared owls. Watch against a full moon for the owl's pale form to appear.

Snowy Owl

Nyctea scandiaca
Length: 24"
Wingspan: 60"

On a bitter cold December day, we walked along the shore at Island Beach State Park. A healthy dune system and a wide white beach beckoned. No snowy owl had been reported yet, but it was certainly time and this was as likely a place as any in New Jersey to see one. After a lengthy walk, we found the remains of a wrecked ship. Smooth curved boards lay exposed in this land of ever-shifting sands. Something was out of place, though—the ship had more to it than we remembered.

That something extra turned out to be a young snowy owl surveying the expanse of beach for a wayward rat. Unlike all other owls, the male and female snowy owl sometimes look decidedly different. The adult male is almost pure white; the adult female is white with some dark barring or flecking (much like an immature male), and the immature female is darkest of all.

Focused on some distant curiosity, this beautiful large white owl raised and lowered its fat, feathered neck, then moved its head to the right, then to the left. In a moment it was off and flying. It dropped onto the beach near the jetty and came up moments later with a rat, half eaten already, with just

the tail dangling out of its mouth. The owl returned to the boat and began its strange, snakelike neck and head movements once again.

The snowy owl is one of the world's largest owls. It is North America's heaviest owl, but not the largest in overall size. Although an Arctic tundra breeder, snowy owls migrate south to the prairie provinces of Canada, the northern plains states and New England each winter to escape the icy weather on their tundra breeding grounds. Some winters, when northern prey is particularly limited, major irruptions of snowy owls take place, bringing them regularly to New Jersey, Pennsylvania and even south into Texas.

In the East, during winter irruptions, snowy owls reside in coastal dunes, on salt marshes or frozen lake shores, in farmland and at airports—all areas that look most like the Arctic tundra above tree line, where these owls are commonly found. New York's Kennedy Airport, Boston's Logan Airport and the Calgary International Airport attract one or more every winter from December through April. In the West, prairies, grasslands and farmed areas attract them, as do lakeshores, harbors and ice-covered lakes and rivers. On the prairies and farmlands of Alberta, Saskatchewan, Manitoba and North Dakota, hundreds of snowy owls, many of them adults, may be found every winter.

One would think that this large white

With a wingspan of nearly five feet, the snowy owl is one of the world's largest owls.

owl that lives and hunts in open spaces would be an easy owl to spot. However, this is not necessarily so. In southern regions, in winter, snowy owls are far less diurnal than they are on their breeding grounds. While you may find a snowy owl active at any time of day, usually they are decidedly crepuscular (most active during the dim hours of dawn and dusk) and are often active during some portion of the night.

If you are seeking snowy owls, search at dawn and in the late afternoon. The owl on the beach mentioned above soon went to roost behind a sand dune, in a slight depression within a tussock of beach grass. It was virtually out of sight there for the rest of the day.

Near Newburyport, Massachusetts, a wildlife drive through the Parker River National Wildlife Refuge at midday produced no snowy owls. The same route at dusk produced five. Snowy owls roost out of sight and out of the wind and cold during midday hours. There are certainly exceptions to this rule, but you can maximize your chances by focusing your efforts early and late in the day.

Scanning is a very important technique for finding snowy owls. Use binoculars and a spotting scope to study every surface on meadows, salt marshes, frozen lakeshores, farmlands and roadside ditches near these habitats. Also study every man-made structure that offers a commanding view of the surrounding feeding habitat—check every fence post, pole, duck blind, hay mound and rock jetty. We have found snowy owls perched on chimneys, rooftops, light stan-

Although they breed in the Arctic, snowy owls migrate to the northern states in the winter.

dards, telephone poles, television antennas and water towers. We saw one memorable New England bird on the same chimney four days in a row. Another bird preferred a condominium rooftop, ignoring dead cedars on the marsh just a short distance away.

Look for white bumps with yellow eyes. Snowys almost always face the sun when roosting. Their breasts will gleam a white or slightly yellowish hue, creating a brilliant reflection. When searching for immature birds, look for a darker object on ice and snow. While waiting for the ferry to southeastern Ontario's Amherst Island, we scanned the off-white frozen surface of Lake Ontario and found a snowy owl perched on the ice. A damp, cold wind ruffled its feathers and two dark pellets were beside it. Be forewarned: you will find at least a few hundred Clorox bottles for every snowy owl you discover, but do not ignore any white blob on marshes or grasslands. The one you do not look at with your binoculars might turn out to be the real thing.

Besides concentrating your efforts at dawn and dusk, you may maximize your chances by knowing when to expect snowy owls. In New Jersey, nine out of ten snowy owls are first found the last week in November or the first two weeks in December. This is when snowy owls arrive and are the most conspicuous, before they have migrated, dispersed or been reduced in numbers by injuries, starvation or shooting.

Snowy owls always make it onto local birding hotlines. If you hear of one, visit the spot as soon as possible. Some snowy owls may be seen for only one or two days, while others may remain all winter.

Lingering birds can become territorial and use the same hunting area and perches week after week. Do not get discouraged if you do not find the bird at first. It took one resident birder five tries before she found a snowy owl reported week after week on the Cape May Birding Hotline.

If the bird is not where it was originally reported, fan out. Check adjacent and nearby suitable habitat. Snowy owls have large winter ranges and may travel two or three miles. They may or may not return to the perch where they were initially spotted.

All of these suggestions are for those who live in areas where snowy owls may appear, even if infrequently. If you live in the southern states, you need to travel to see snowy owls. Newburyport, Massachusetts, is a reliable place to start your search. We have seen as many as thirteen and as few as one, but we have never missed seeing a snowy owl there over

President's Day weekend in February during our annual pilgrimage. If you are unfamiliar with the area, there are several excellent bird-finding guides for eastern Massachusetts and New England. Snowy owl sightings and directions are generally on the Boston birding hotline (617-259-8805). Almost any winter one or more snowy owls can be seen at Parker River National Wildlife Refuge or Salisbury Beach State Park, particularly if you drive the roads in early morning and late afternoon. This area is one of the easiest and most accessible and comfortable places in the nation to see snowy owls.

Another snowy owl hotspot is Point Peninsula in northern New York on the northeast shore of Lake Ontario, above Watertown, New York. This area and the area northeast along the St. Lawrence Sea-

During winter irruptions, snowy owls can be spotted in many areas across the northern states.

way to Massena Dam attracts numbers of snowy owls each winter, even when they are comparatively scarce elsewhere. Braddock Bay Raptor Research runs winter trips to this area to enjoy snowy and short-eared owls and rough-legged hawks. The eastern Upper Peninsula in Michigan, especially the Sault Ste. Marie area, is also excellent for spotting snowy owls and other owls and hawks. Whitefish Point Bird Observatory monitors winter raptor numbers and distribution and offers winter tours in this area. The Duluth, Minnesota/Superior, Wisconsin, harbor also has a few snowy owls wintering from November through March every year. Call the Duluth birding hotline for details (218-525-5952).

Active during the day and a creature of open country, the burrowing owl is one of the easiest to spot.

Burrowing Owl

Athene cunicularia
Length: 10"
Wingspan: 23"

The burrowing owl is one of the easiest owls to spot since it is active during the day and it is an owl of open country. To search for burrowing owls, you must use different techniques than those used for most other owls. Open prairies and grasslands need to be scanned. Check each slightly elevated area for something out of place, particularly fence posts, which are highly favored perches. In the West, check both active and abandoned prairie dog towns for burrowing owls. Near the Salton Sea, in southern California, burrowing owls nest on the spoil banks created when irrigation ditches are dug.

Burrowing owls usually perch in daylight at the entrance to their underground nest sites. They do not really burrow, but usually nest in abandoned dens originally dug by prairie dogs, ground squirrels, badgers, skunks, armadillos and foxes. One or several pairs may nest on the outskirts of an active ground squirrel or prairie dog colony. Often they sit on posts or mounds near the nest opening. With good seasonal timing, you may see the downy young looking out from the burrow entrance. If you find them during the day, come back at dusk to watch them hunting and maybe to hear them calling.

Burrowing owls are westerners, found from the plains states west to California. They are migratory, ranging as far north as the Canadian prairies of Alberta in summer, but withdrawing south to Texas and Arizona in winter. This migratory habit has caused a few burrowing owls to turn up as vagrants in some unexpected places, such as New Haven, Connecticut, Long Island, New York, and Cape Hatteras, North Carolina.

The only eastern population of burrowing owls is a nonmigratory race in southern Florida. Here they are often quite easy to find. *A Birder's Guide to Florida* by James Lane, revised by Harold Holt, gives excellent directions to a number of burrowing owl colony sites.

The easiest places in Florida to find these owls is on the golf courses and airports of the Florida Keys. The Marathon airport has been an excellent place to sight them in recent years. Recently, a burrow has been used right next to the terminal building. Also check the Marathon golf course. The Key West airport and the Homestead airport usually hold burrowing owls too.

Burrowing owlets often stand outside their burrows.

Northern Pygmy Owl

Glaucidium gnoma
Length: 7"
Wingspan: 15"

We were climbing Mount Pinos in Los Padres National Forest, California. We were not searching for owls but were instead determined to see the last California condors before they disappeared from the wild, perhaps forever. To this end, we scanned the skies from every opening along the forest road and trails, finding "only" golden eagles.

We reached the snow line, and debated climbing further, but chose to wait where we had a good overview of the sky and canyons. Owls were the last thing on our minds, but even the most obsessed would-be condor watcher could not ignore the incessant racket of mountain chickadees. Then Steller's jays joined in, and even a Clark's nutcracker flew in to investigate. These songbirds were mobbing something, but we couldn't quite get a look. A revolving ball of feathers fell from the pines overhead and bounced off the snow—the source of the turmoil. A pygmy owl had attacked a western kingbird. It was a life and death struggle in the snow at our feet. We watched, transfixed, as the birds rolled over and over in the snow. Finally, the pygmy owl flew up to a branch overhead.

We realized it was hard to tell the back of the owl's head from the front. Only the glaring yellow eyes differentiated the face from the black false eyespots, which seemed to look at us from the back of the head. The owl flew deeper into the forest, the mobbing songbirds marking its path. The kingbird? Exhausted but alive, it picked itself up and flew weakly away. The condors? Well, we had forgotten about them for a while, but finally found them the next day near Tejon Pass—twelve together, ending a week of searching that had led to so many rewards—many of them totally unexpected.

For us, this pygmy owl encounter was an example of one invaluable outdoor lesson. You will not necessarily see what you are looking for, but if you pay your dues and put in your time outdoors, you will see something equally exciting.

Pygmy owls are chiefly diurnal, but most active at dawn and dusk. They will, however, fly, hunt and call at night as well. On this same trip, one

Look for cavity-nesting pygmy owls in dense woodlands in foothills, mountains and canyon bottoms.

An aggressive predator, the pygmy owl is diurnal, but most active at dawn and dusk.

called incessantly near our campground for as long as we were awake. Each spring and fall a few may sing during the day for long periods of time. Look for pygmy owls in dense woodlands in foothills, mountains and canyon bottoms. The northern pygmy owl is found from Alaska south through Mexico, but only at higher elevations.

An aggressive predator, this species is perhaps more frequently mobbed by songbirds than any other owl—so listen for the constant, strident, scolding calls of songbirds. Let them locate the owl for you.

Otherwise, search dense evergreens for their perched silhouettes. Pygmy owls may also sit out exposed on bare trees or power lines, particularly near dusk.

Tapes are a tool for the pygmy owl spotter and can be tried day or night. If a tape attracts curious songbirds, it is likely that pygmy owls are present since the songbirds are familiar with the calls on the tape. Once at midday, while doing a whistled imitation of the pygmy owl's call to attract songbirds, we had a distant but distinct pygmy owl answer us repeatedly.

Ferruginous Pygmy Owl

Glaucidium brasilianum
Length: 6"
Wingspan: 15"

We had been out for three nights straight and had heard ferruginous pygmy owls each night. We even heard one calling in the midafternoon. Each time, however, we failed to find the owl. Either some other bird encounter intervened or the vegetation was too thick. Tapes had even failed to bring the bird in. We could hear it, but we were probably outside its defended territory. It would not move closer, and a wall of thorny bushes prevented a closer approach.

Finally, we heard one calling from a deciduous tree standing alone in an open grassy field. Even when our group surrounded the tree, the owl continued calling. Switching on flashlights, we began to search. The call seemed ventriloquistic. Five minutes passed, then ten. No owl. Finally, our guide said, "I've got it" and held the beam of the flashlight on the bird. From that angle it was sitting out in plain sight, but it had taken fifteen minutes to find the right angle. Even while held in the flashlight beam, it contin-

Rare in North America, the ferruginous pygmy owl is common in Central and South America.

ued to call. We set spotting scopes up on the bird, and half an hour later we left, satiated. The bird continued to give its rapid repeated call as we drove off into the night, leaving it to its task of attracting a mate.

The ferruginous pygmy owl is uncommon in North America, but common from central Mexico southward through much of South America. In fact, the encounter described above took place at a Venezuelan ranch. In the United States, ferruginous pygmy owls replace northern pygmy owls in lower elevations. They are rare, and only found in specific areas in southern Texas, such as along the Rio Grande Valley in riparian woodlands, and in southern Arizona, where they are found in saguaro cacti and mesquite thicket desert areas.

Like the closely allied northern pygmy owl, the ferruginous pygmy owl is chiefly diurnal, yet crepuscular (most active near dawn and dusk). Also, like the northern pygmy, its wing beats are unmuffled because the primary feathers lack a serrated leading edge. Ferruginous owls, too, commonly feed on songbirds.

When searching for the ferruginous pygmy owl, use techniques similar to those employed in searches for the northern pygmy owl. Listen for them in June when they are very vocal, calling day and night. Tapes or repeated imitations of their rapid call should elicit a response, but be patient. It may take considerable time to attract a bird and even longer to find it once it is lured. Remember, pygmy owls are only 6 inches long, and that includes the tail (which is uncommonly long for an owl).

Elf Owl

Micrathene whitneyi
Length: 5½"
Wingspan: 15"

It had been a long drive — 36 hours nonstop from New Jersey to Attwater Prairie Chicken National Wildlife Refuge. After a foggy dawn at the lek (mating ground) and a morning at the refuge, it was another eight hours south to Bentsen Rio Grande State Park, our home for a week while exploring the valley. Bentsen State Park, a fabled birding spot on the Rio Grande River, hosts many Mexican species that rarely make it into the United States.

After so many hours on the road, we were thinking more about our sleeping bags than about spotting rare birds. And frankly, the last thing on our mind was owls. As we made camp, quite a few birders wandered by, many pausing to search the treetops above our campsite. Oddly, birders began to gather as we cooked dinner, until eventually they formed a semicircle around our campsite and seemed to be waiting for something. Just as we were about to ask what they were looking for, a flashlight-toting man strode into our campsite and loudly announced, "We really don't see why you had to camp under it. You could have camped down the road, like the rest of us. You're no doubt keeping it from coming

out!" His indignant attitude was a shock after our 44-hour drive, and we had no idea what he was talking about.

In fact, we found out, we were camped under a tree with a cavity that several elf owls were living in, right over campsite 137. We quickly wrapped up dinner, joined what was then a small crowd, and saw our very first elf owls. The lessons in owl spotting here are twofold. If we had called the local birding hotline, we would have learned of the elf owls over our campsite, which were spotted every night just before dark.

Once common, elf owls, *above and left*, are thought to be declining throughout much of their range.

In all truthfulness, we did not see the owls very well. As soon as the first one peeked out of its hole, it was greeted by a loudly shouted, "There it is!" and immediately hit with 12 flashlight beams. As it flushed and flew off through the campground, about 20 birders followed, led by the fellow who had confronted us and was now shouting very loudly, "Over here, I have the light on it." As the throng moved off, crashing through the campground in pursuit of the owl, silence returned to our owlless campsite. For the next several hours, individual birders came and went, all shining their beams on the tree cavity over our tent.

Hotlines can be very helpful when locating rare birds, owls included. But in more than one case, repeated viewing by numbers of people have driven birds away. The potential for harassment is something every birder should always keep in mind. In this case, a quiet group using perhaps just one light might have had a better view and disturbed the owl far less. Six months later we heard that the owl was no longer being seen at site 137. While no single person disturbed the elf owls, the cumulative impact of many birders, night after night, forced it to find a more peaceful place to raise its family.

Elf owls, at 5½ inches, are North America's smallest owl. Once common in oak-sycamore canyons and streamsides, as well as foothills and desert areas (where it nests in cavities in saguaro cacti and utility poles), the elf owl population is now thought to be declining in much of its former range. Although found from extreme southern Texas to extreme southeastern California, it is numerous only in southern Arizona.

The elf owl is a migrant, leaving the

United States and northern Mexico in late October and not returning until March or later. While it is largely nocturnal, it is once in a while seen at dawn or dusk.

Elf owls do not respond well to tapes or imitations of their calls. But for a brief period in early spring (late April and early May), they are very vocal. Familiarize yourself with their chattering calls and, during this period, put time into listening for them at dawn and dusk. Patiently and quietly wait at their saguaro cacti and tree cavity roosts for a glimpse at dusk. Do not neglect full moons for a better look. Modern binoculars with good light-gathering capabilities perform quite well on moonlit nights. With luck (preparation plus opportunity) you, too, may see an elf owl peering out of its saguaro cactus home.

North America's smallest owl, with a length of less than six inches, the elf owl nests in holes in cacti.

Northern Hawk Owl

Surnia ulula
Length: 15"
Wingspan: 33"

Early in our birding careers, we decided we had to see a hawk owl. We knew that we were going to have to travel. But even so, over a period of a few years, we passed up several opportunities that were within reasonable driving distance. Our friend Jim Dowdell went to see one in New York State that he lamented, "just sat there all day, [and] never flew or anything." Another friend, owl researcher Patti Hodgetts, went to see one in southern Maine that she described as "living on the cloverleaf of a highway exit, in the middle of a town, with too much traffic to enjoy it." With these case histories, we did not feel we had missed too much.

However, one cold January night in 1988, our friend Dave Sibley called from Connecticut to ask us if we wanted to venture to Eastport, Maine, with him, where a hawk owl had been sighted for a couple of weeks, and, according to the hotline, as recently as that morning. It took a few days to clear the decks, but the following Saturday we met Dave in New Haven, spent an entire after-

The northern hawk owl is a bird of the deep spruce forests and tamarack bogs.

noon watching a black gyrfalcon there (a good start to the trip!) and then headed north for Eastport.

The next morning, armed with a predawn breakfast, lots of warm clothes and directions from the local Christmas Count compiler, we headed out of town to Leighton Neck. Ten minutes later, we pulled up to the spot. The owl was perched on a telephone pole, busily watching for prey in the snowy landscape.

This owl chase was educational from a number of standpoints. The hotline told us about the bird. A local expert willingly gave us updated directions. And, we chose our first hawk owl carefully. It was hunting in one of the most scenic areas in the country, far better than a highway cloverleaf. Moreover, it was not a marathon chase.

Fortunately we were able to take five days off, and we learned about hawk owls for the next three days. We studied it as it hunted, caught prey, fed, passed pellets and drove off crows. We watched it fly, hover and preen. Dave sketched and painted it. Aside from the local bird count compiler, we never saw another birder. Some had checked off the hawk owl after viewing it

for only a few minutes. They learned very little about hawk owl behavior and natural history.

The moral of this story is, if possible, to pick your birds carefully. The Eastport bird was spectacular, in part because of its surroundings. Pine grosbeaks and Bohemian waxwings perched in the trees over the owl, and bald eagles circled in off the bay. It was a very satisfying hawk owl experience. We have since seen hawk owls in Pennsylvania and Michigan, where we saw four, but, somehow, the first one was the best.

The hawk owl is a bird of the far northern forests. It primarily breeds north of the lower 48 states, from Newfoundland west through Alaska. It is a bird of deep spruce forests and tamarack bogs. Largely nonmigratory, it does withdraw in winter from the northernmost parts of its range. Each winter, one or more vagrants show up in the northern United States, usually in Minnesota, Michigan, New York or Maine. Only once in a great while do we see what could be called a true invasion of this species to the south. Over 160 were recorded during the winter of 1991-92 in Minnesota. Caused by a lack of prey in their northern home, these southern invasions give birders their best chance to see the hawk owl.

Listen to regional hotlines. Often when found, a hawk owl will remain in the area, enabling even those who must come from afar to plan a trip to see it. Follow directions

Largely nonmigratory, hawk owls primarily breed north of the lower 48 states.

closely and call local experts when possible for updates.

When you get to the site, scan widely. In winter, the hawk owl is a bird of open or semiopen country. It usually chooses a high perch overlooking a good feeding habitat. Look on treetops or even telephone poles or wires for its long-tailed silhouette. Sometimes it may perch low in scrub if it is not hunting or if that is all that is available, but generally it prefers height. Often it perches on the edge of open forests or woodlots.

A hawk owl looks much like a perched American kestrel, and it sometimes hovers like a kestrel. Its flight is swift and low—hawklike. On the wing, look for something resembling a Cooper's hawk. If it is quiet and you are fortunate, listen for the mellow warbling call, which to us resembles that of a screech owl. Tapes have been used on breeding territory surveys for hawk owl, but will be completely unnecessary on the wintering grounds.

Hawk owls are diurnal, but seem to be more active early and late in the day. They possibly hunt in darkness, since in their Arctic habitat daylight is so limited during the winter.

If you want to see a hawk owl, you must be flexible. When you hear of a sighting within a reasonable distance, particularly in a scenic area, plan a trip to see it. Take a few days to enjoy both the bird and the natural history of the north. Go for it as soon as possible, because it may be ten years before you get another chance to enjoy this classic Arctic wanderer south of its usually high northern home.

Further Information

OWL BOOKS

Bent, Arthur Cleveland. *Life Histories of North American Birds of Prey,* Vol. 2. Dover Publications, Inc.: New York. 1961. Based on firsthand experiences from researchers all over North America who corresponded with Bent in the 1800s and early 1900s. Though dated, *Life Histories* contains the answers to many questions about owls because the early researchers were highly interested in natural history and behavior. Educational photographs of nest sites.

Bunn, D. S., A. B. Warburton and R. D. S. Wilson. *The Barn Owl.* Buteo Books: Vermillion, South Dakota. 1982. A classic work on barn owls based on nearly 40 years of field work in Britain, the United States and Europe. Complemented by wonderful illustrations by Ian Willis.

Burton, John A. (ed.). *Owls of the World.* 2nd edition, Tanager Books: Dover, New Hampshire. 1984. Range maps, illustrations and photographs; a chapter on pellets with extremely helpful comparative and composition photographs and a detailed description of each of the owl voices.

Cameron, Angus and Peter Parnall. *The Nightwatchers.* Four Winds Press: New York. 1971. Filled with vivid descriptions and anecdotes. Illustrated with striking black-and-white line drawings by Peter Parnall.

Clark, Richard J., Dwight Smith and Leon Kelso. *Working Bibliography of Owls of the World.* National Wildlife Federation. 1978. A little dated but still a useful guide to the scientific owl literature.

Connor, Jack. *The Complete Birder.* Houghton Mifflin: Boston. 1988. If you like owls but are new to birdwatching, this book is packed with valuable information about one of the favorite pastimes in North America.

Craighead, John J. and Frank C. *Hawks, Owls and Wildlife.* Dover Publications,

Inc.: New York. 1969. A classic study of predatory-prey ecology.

de la Torre, Julio. *Owls, Their Life and Behavior*. Crown Publishers, Inc.: New York. 1990. Engaging text by de la Torre and spectacular photographs by Art Wolfe.

Eckert, Allan W. *The Owls of North America*. Weathervane Books: New York. 1987. Good scientific summary and good information on subspecies.

Ehrlich, Paul, David Dobkin and Darryl Wheye. *The Birder's Handbook, A Field Guide to the Natural History of North American Birds*. Simon & Schuster, Inc.: New York. 1988. This book is like having a naturalist along with you sharing a steady stream of fascinating and little-known facts. The essays relating to owls are superb: "How Owls Hunt in the Dark," "Pellets," "Irruptions," "What Do Birds Hear?," "Mobbing," "Courtship Feeding," "Site Tenacity" and a number of others.

Holmgren, Virginia C. *Owls in Folklore and Natural History*. Capra Press: Santa Barbara, California. 1988. A fun read!

Hume, Rob. *Owls of the World*. Running Press: Philadelphia. 1991. This book covers each of the 148 species found around the globe, with beautiful illustrations by Trevor Boyer. Very helpful distribution maps.

Johnsgard, Paul A. *North American Owls, Biology and Natural History*. Smithsonian Institution Press: Washington, D.C. 1988. A comprehensive study; detailed accounts of the lives of each of our owls. Range maps and wonderful illustrations.

Mikkola, Heimo. *Owls of Europe*. Buteo Books: Vermillion, South Dakota. 1983. This major work reviews the 13 owls that breed in Europe as well as four species found in North Africa and the Middle East. Complemented by wonderful illustrations by Ian Willis, as well as photographs and maps.

Nero, Robert W. *The Great Gray Owl*. Smithsonian Institution Press: Washington, D.C. 1980. A classic work on great gray owls by the man who has studied them extensively. The reader is transported into this owl's often remote world.

Quinton, Michael S. *Ghost of the Forest, The Great Gray Owl*. Northland Press: Flagstaff, Arizona. 1988. A striking photographic essay on the great gray owl.

Terres, John K. *The Audubon Society Encyclopedia of North American Birds*. Wings Books: New York. 1991. This beautiful and highly informative book is a must for any library. Write-ups are concise, thorough and filled with fascinating natural history information.

Toops, Connie. *The Enchanting Owl*. Voyageur Press: Stillwater, Minnesota. 1990. Excellent introduction to owls; includes wonderful photographs.

Tyler, Hamilton A. and Don Phillips. *Owls by Day and Night*. Naturegraph Publishers, Inc.: Happy Camp, California. 1978. An informative and insightful book covering North America's owls, including many fascinating and site-specific first-hand experiences.

Walker, Louis Wayne. *The Book of Owls*. University of Texas Press: Austin, Texas. 1993. This is our all-time favorite book about owls. Full of fascinating anecdotes about and descriptions of firsthand experiences with owls by "America's premier owl watcher." Very lively reading. Complemented by nearly 100 highly educational photographs. This book, which was originally published in 1978, was out of print until the University of Texas Press reprinted it.

Yolen, Jane. *Owl Moon*. Philomel Books: New York. 1988. This is our favorite children's storybook. It is about a little girl who goes out owling with her father. It is beautifully illustrated by John Schoenherr, and it makes a great gift for any child. I think the parents enjoy it just as much and hopefully follow it through by taking their children out owling.

Zoobooks 2. *Owls*. Wildlife Education, Ltd., 930 West Washington Street, San Diego, California 92103. 1985. Written for children, this book is beautifully illustrated and presents information on owls in an easy-to-understand manner. A good learning tool for children of all ages.

OWL SONGS AND CALLS

A Field Guide to Bird Songs of Eastern & Central North America (Peterson Field Guide Series). Roger T. Peterson (ed.). 1983. Two cassettes or one compact disc.

A Field Guide to Western Bird Songs. Cornell Laboratory. 1992. Three cassettes or two compact discs with booklet. Keyed to Peterson's revised *Field Guide to Western Birds*.

Guide to Bird Sounds. Cornell Laboratory. 1985. Two cassettes. Keyed to National Geographic Society's *Field Guide to the Birds of North America*.

Voices of New World Owls by J. W. Hardy, B. B. Coffey, Jr. and G. B. Reynard. 1989. One cassette.

Bird Songs of Southeast Arizona and Southern Texas by Geoffrey A. Keller. 1988. One record or one cassette.

Birding by Ear, A Guide to Bird Song Identification: Eastern/Central (Peterson Field Guide Series) by Richard K. Walton and Robert W. Lawson. 1989. Three cassettes and booklet. Excellent teaching tool to help you learn ways to identify and remember bird songs.

Birding by Ear, A Guide to Bird Song Identification: Western (Peterson Field Guide Series), by Richard K. Walton and Robert W. Lawson. 1990. Three cassettes and booklet. Also excellent, with focus on western birds.

LEARN FROM THE EXPERTS

Barn Owl Research Foundation, P.O. Box 680183, San Antonio, TX 78238. Most intensive adult population barn owl study in the world, under way in southwestern New Jersey since 1980. Annual report sent to supporters.

Braddock Bay Raptor Research, 432 Manitou Beach Road, Hilton, NY 14468. Phone: (716) 392-5685. Spring migration hotspot on southern shore of Lake Ontario. Migrant saw-whet, long-eared and short-eared owls have been banded here each spring since 1986; boreal owl also possible. Newsletter, *The Raptor Researcher*, published biannually. Owl Walks offered at dusk on Saturdays and Sundays from mid-March to the first of May. "Bird of Prey Week" scheduled each year for late April; includes some owl activities. Winter bird trips offered to Point Peninsula for snowy and short-eared owls and rough-legged hawks.

Cape May Bird Observatory, New Jersey Audubon Society, 707 E. Lake Drive, Cape May Point, NJ 08212. Phone: (609) 884-2736; Birding Hotline: (609) 884-2626. Newsletter, *Peregrine Observer*, is published twice each year. Fall migration hotspot on East Coast. Migrant long-eared, barn and saw-whet owls have been

banded here each fall since 1969. Organized "Sunset Birding Walks" and "Night Watch" walks offered at peak of fall migration; owls may be sighted (mid-September through November), but outings focus on all nocturnal migrants, with owls being a real bonus! "Owl Package Specials," offered in January (and sometimes February), feature an owl workshop/slide show on owl habits and habitats followed by a field trip in search of wintering owls. Short-eared owls are almost always seen.

Hawk Ridge Research Station, managed by Duluth Audubon Society, c/o Biology Department, University of Minnesota, Duluth, MN 55812. Fall migration hotspot on southwest shore of Lake Superior. *Hawk Ridge Annual Report* covers fall hawk watch report and daily totals, hawk and owl banding station report and monthly totals, the passerine banding report and totals and news of upcoming birding weekends and events. A "Boreal Owl Birding Weekend" is offered each year in either late March or early April to Superior National Forest (northeast of Duluth), where boreal owls breed. Saw-whets are also often sighted and sometimes great grays, northern hawk owls and long-eared owls. This weekend and other Minnesota birding weekends are co-sponsored by the Minnesota Ornithologist's Union and Hawk Ridge Nature Reserve. For more information contact Kim Eckert at the address given above or call (218) 525-6930.

Whitefish Point Bird Observatory,

Whitefish Point Road, Box 115, Paradise, MI 49768. (906) 492-3596. A newsletter, *The Migrant*, is published in March, July and November. This area is a spring migration hotspot on the southeast shore of Lake Superior. Migrant saw-whet, long-eared and boreal owls have been banded here each spring (in April and May) since 1983. Small numbers of each species are banded here in the fall as well (in October and early November). Organized owl watches, "The Evening Flight," are offered from mid-April to mid-May to spot and identify owl migrants. Winter research is conducted on great grays, hawk owls and snowy owls in the Upper Peninsula, north of Whitefish Point. Observatory-sponsored winter tours, based in the Sault Ste. Marie area, are offered from early January to early March that focus on winter raptors, including snowy, great gray and hawk owls.

TRAVEL

Buff, Sheila. *The Birder's Sourcebook, A Compendium of Essential Birding Information*. 1994. Lyons & Burford, Publishers: NY, NY. Excellent source of birding products, places and organizations.

Lane, James A. *A Birder's Guide to . . .* (any one of 6 separate booklets: *Southeast Arizona, Southern California, Colorado, Florida, Rio Grande Valley, Texas Coast*). ABA/Lane Series. Since the death of James Lane, many of these guides have been updated by other authors.

American Birding Association (ABA), P.O. Box 6599, Colorado Springs, CO 80934. (800) 634-7736.

1. Newsletter, *Winging It*, published monthly, normally includes a birder's guide to a little known hotspot in North America, details on good birds from the previous month's hotlines around North America, an up-to-date list of all "Rare Bird Alert" (birding hotlines) phone numbers in North America and a variety of other articles.

2. *ABA Sales Annotated Catalog and Price List* offers a complete list of regional birding guides (arranged state by state for the United States, province by province for Canada and country by country for the rest of the world), sound recordings and optics and accessories for mail-order purchase.

3. *Birding*, published bimonthly, often includes thorough reviews of bird books and sound recordings. Also the "Tools of the Trade" article about equipment is usually very helpful.

American Birds, 700 Broadway, NY, NY 10003. (212) 979-3000. Five publications each year (spring, summer, fall, winter and Christmas Bird Count issues) annotate seasonal bird records around the country. The Christmas Bird Count issue includes the results of over 1,500 counts across the country. High-count areas are listed for each species, making it a quick way to learn where the best places are to see any particular species.

Photography and Illustration Credits

PATRICIA AND CLAY SUTTON
17, 18, 21 bottom, 32, 33, 35 left & right, 38, 39, 42 top & bottom, 44 left & right, 49 top & bottom, 58 top & bottom, 60, 62, 63, 64, 67, 70, 73, 83, 101, 112, 114, 118.

ART WOLFE
6, 11, 13, 16, 22, 30, 40, 45, 46, 47, 51, 53, 54, 61, 68, 69, 72, 74-75, 82, 84, 85 top & bottom, 88, 96, 97 left & right, 103, 104, 109, 110, 113, 116, 120, 121, 122, 123, 127, 128, 129, back cover: top left & right.

BILL BYRNE
20, 36, 65, 77, 89, 90, 91, 106.

RON AUSTING
Front cover, 9, 12, 19, 23, 24, 25, 26, 28, 31, 43, 48, 52, 56, 57, 71, 78, 79, 81, 86, 93, 94, 98, 100, 105, 108, 124, 126, 132, back cover: bottom right.

JOHN SHAW
14-15, back cover: bottom left.

ROD PLANCK
21 top, 119, 130.

RANGE MAPS
Created by Eugenie Seidenberg Delaney; continent outline by Roberta Cooke.

Index

About the Authors

PATRICIA TAYLOR SUTTON is the Teacher Naturalist at New Jersey Audubon Society's Cape May Bird Observatory. Formerly, she was Senior Naturalist at Cape May Point State Park. In these two positions, she has taught thousands about the wonders of owls. She is the author of New Jersey Audubon Society's publication *Backyard Habitat for Birds, a Guide for Landowners and Communities in New Jersey.*

Clay Sutton is a wildlife biologist and staff ornithologist for Herpetological Associates, an environmental consulting firm specializing in threatened and endangered species protection. His job often involves finding owls. He is a co-author, with Pete Dunne and Dave Sibley, of *Hawks in Flight.*

The Suttons live near Cape May, New Jersey, with an English setter, a dalmation and a pair of screech owls in their overgrown backyard.